IDENTITY-BASED STUDENT ACTIVISM

Historically and contemporarily, student activists have worked to address oppression on college and university campuses. This book explores the experiences of students engaged in identity-based activism today as it relates to racism, sexism, homophobia, transphobia, ableism, and other forms of oppression. Grounded by a national study on student activism and the authors' combined 40 years of experience working in higher education, *Identity-Based Student Activism* uses a critical, power-conscious lens to unpack the history of identity-based activism, relationships between activists and administrators, and student activism as labor. This book provides an opportunity for administrators, educators, faculty, and student activists to reflect on their current ideas and behaviors around activism and consider new ways for improving their relationships with each other, and ultimately, their campus climates.

Chris Linder is an assistant professor of higher education at the University of Utah, USA.

Stephen John Quaye is an associate professor of higher education and student affairs at The Ohio State University, USA, and an associate editor of the *Journal of Diversity in Higher Education*.

Alex C. Lange is a doctoral student of higher education and student affairs at the University of Iowa, USA.

Meg E. Evans is a doctoral student of student affairs administration at the University of Georgia, USA.

Terah J. Stewart is an assistant professor of student affairs and higher education at Iowa State University, USA.

IDENTITY-BASED STUDENT ACTIVISM

Power and Oppression on College Campuses

Chris Linder, Stephen John Quaye, Alex C. Lange, Meg E. Evans, and Terah J. Stewart

LONDON AND NEW YORK

First published 2020
by Routledge
52 Vanderbilt Avenue, New York, NY 10017

and by Routledge
2 Park Square, Milton Park, Abingdon, Oxon, OX14 4RN

Routledge is an imprint of the Taylor & Francis Group, an informa business

Library of Congress Cataloging-in-Publication Data
A catalog record for this book has been requested

ISBN: 978-0-367-18294-6 (hbk)
ISBN: 978-0-367-18295-3 (pbk)
ISBN: 978-0-429-06058-8 (ebk)

Typeset in Bembo
by Apex CoVantage, LLC

Printed in Canada

To Cori Bazemore-James, Taylor Cain, Marvette Lacy,

Wilson Kwamogi Okello, Ricky Ericka Roberts, and Erin Weston.

This book is a result of several years of labor dating back to August of 2016. As is often the case with large voluntary research teams, researchers' participation will be fluid and targeted, and not every member of the team will be part of every developed project from study data. However, we want to also acknowledge all members, past and present, of the #ActivismOnCampus research team for your time, talent, and treasure.

Thank you.

CONTENTS

FOREWORD

When a professor of ethnic studies on campus introduced me to Black radical organizing in college in 2009, I could have never predicted that just a few years later I would become one of the founders of Black Lives Matter Atlanta, a chapter of the Black Lives Matter Global Network. I never envisioned that I would be continuing the fight in the Black liberation tradition that spans from the battle of fighting slavery and colonization on the continent of Africa to the civil rights movement. I, among many others, have continued the collective sacrifice for global equity. In finding my life's work in social justice I began a career in higher education working in identity-based offices to provide diversity, inclusion, and equity programming and training across campus. I met the authors of this text through working in colleges and universities with the deliberate intention of disrupting the normative ways universities navigate and avoid transphobia, sexism, racism, ableism, and power.

In this book, the authors use interviews from 25 activists on college campuses to take a deeper look into the students' experiences while also interrogating their own privilege as educators. The narratives captured help readers better understand the labor and sacrifice students make in an attempt to improve their campus policies and environment for students on the margins. Through the impressive and intricate interweaving of the student narratives, the authors made clear a consistent struggle, and holistic view in the new generation of freedom fighters. One of the issues the authors make alarmingly apparent is how students sacrifice their mental, emotional, financial, and academic well-being by choosing bravery and survival when many faculty and staff members of the institution protect themselves or the university over the students and their safety. It also becomes clear how students are often re-traumatized by campus officials in the attempt to hold the institution accountable in their commitment of being student-centered and welcoming to everyone. Rachel, a participant in the study, shared the systematic stress of going through a traumatic incident, experiencing vicarious trauma through the narrative of someone who also experienced the trauma, and then organizing to fight the issues through hours of meetings. Thereafter, students would attempt to receive mental health support on the issues and found that counselors were unequipped to understand and help them effectively navigate the magnitude of harm that comes with being an activist. The authors give us a view of what student activists on college campuses have cycled through, year after year, with little to no systematic change.

Identity Based Student Activism: Power and Oppression on College Campuses is an offering to educators in higher education who have witnessed the rise of student activism over the last several years and understand that this is simply the beginning. For example, Black students on the campus of the University of Missouri organized and successfully ousted the president. Student activism, as well as the national discourse on race and police brutality, inclusivity of trans and non-binary folks, and resistance to anti-immigration laws, have awakened the fears of some Administrators. As a result, they are now considering taking a proactive approach to the consistent demands of an ever-growing diverse, aware, and socially conscious population of students. The authors have brilliantly developed an intersectional analysis about the ways student activists interrogate and demand change from their universities, and, ultimately, the authors determine true transformation begins with demanding that higher education administrators and educators start to engage and question their own privilege and identity in this historical moment. The authors themselves model the way by naming early in the text their positionality and journey to awakening on issues centering their own misguidedness and growth about racism, sexism, ableism, homophobia, and power.

In my own journey, I have grown from the president of the Black Student Union at a predominantly white, mid-size, public university to becoming an administrator with the dream of fostering a new generation of activists in the ways I was led (and misled) by faculty and staff. I soon had that dream extinguished. As an administrator, I experienced many of the challenges shared in this book by campus staff members who experienced isolation, punishment, and a warring of the spirit. I was often left in the middle to either serve the university's agenda by hosting multicultural programs to quiet the demands of students dealing with real issues of discrimination and harassment on campus or support the student activists who demanded the university create systematic change and space for them. Every time I chose to serve and represent the students and every time, I was punished. I began to be known as the radical staff member who would not be promoted for fear that I would go rogue. With this book, the authors helped me not feel isolated but imbued with pride that I decided to be on the right side of history fighting for our collective freedom and not our individual professional or financial safety.

The authors give us a road map to begin to interrogate ourselves and the sanctity of higher education. Historically, we are aware that universities were created for cisgender, straight, white men and were never intended for People of Color or for low-income, disabled, LGBTQ, and Indigenous people to attend. The authors demand that we no longer hold on to the old scripts of diversity but truly engage students to envision and create a new world where the labor of including marginalized students is not left to the students to cure.

In forthright speech Audre Lorde (1984) said, "For the master's tools will never dismantle the master's house. They may allow us to temporarily beat him at his own game but will never enable us to bring about genuine change" (p. 112). *Identity-Based Student Activism: Power and Oppression on College Campuses* demands that we no longer play the game that has kept us shackled to the institution's old ways of being, but begin to create the tools that will build a new house for its new inhabitants and will subsequently get us all free us all.

Tiffany R. Smith
Senior Coordinator, Multicultural Services and Programs,
University of Georgia

PREFACE

College students have engaged in activism since the early colonial colleges (Geiger, 2016; Horowitz, 1987; Rudolph, 1990; Thelin, 2011). Although early student activism focused primarily on students' concerns about their living conditions, food, and classically oriented curriculum (Rudolph, 1990), over time student activists started to raise awareness about injustices in the larger culture, including anti-war protests, racism and sexism in higher education, and student privacy rights (Astin, Astin, Bayer, & Bisconti, 1975). Throughout history, student activism has been responsive to what is happening in the world and to students' specific identities and contexts. Although college and university campuses frequently serve as sites of oppression and reproduction of the oppression that exists in the larger culture, they may also serve as sites of resistance against oppression.

The purpose of this book is to focus specifically on identity-based activism and illustrate the unique challenges and outcomes of identity-based activism. Taking together the findings of a national study on student activism and the authors' combined 40 years of experience working in higher education, we provide insight for student activists, educators, and administrators about the role of power and dominance in campus-based student activism. Different from other texts on student activism, in this book, we intentionally and unapologetically center identity, power, and dominance in our analysis. The book is not simply about student activism—it is about identity-based student activism related to racism, sexism, homophobia, transphobia, ableism, and other forms of oppression. We use a critical, power-conscious lens to illustrate ways students engaged in activism related to minoritized identities contribute to improving campus climates through their labor. Further, we interrogate labels and traditional notions of what constitutes activism as a strategy to validate and support current student activists. Finally, we share strategies for educators and administrators to engage more effectively with and learn from student activists on their campuses.

Intended Audiences

This book provides an opportunity for administrators, educators, and student activists to reflect on their current ideas and behaviors around activism and consider new ways for improving their relationships with each other, and ultimately, improving campus climates related to equity. College and university administrators and educators, including student affairs educators, may benefit from the information shared in this book. Educators may make connections between the stories shared in this book and their experiences on their own campuses, illuminating new strategies for engaging with and supporting identity-based student activists. Further, student activists themselves may benefit from this text; by reading the stories of other activists, they might feel less isolated and gain new strategies for effectively influencing their campus environments.

Additionally, this text may be appropriate for courses in higher education and student affairs graduate preparation programs. Faculty members in some programs have begun to offer electives on student activism and social movements, and this book would be an excellent addition to those programs. This book would enable faculty to engage graduate students in dialogues about ways to support activists, as well as enable students to reflect on their own activism. Further, the book highlights some aspects of college student development theory and organization and administration of higher education, topics covered in several courses in higher education graduate programs at both the master's and the doctoral levels. This text may also be appropriate for social movements courses offered through departments of sociology or identity-related courses offered through women's studies, ethnic studies, or queer studies departments. Finally, the book may also be useful in first-year seminar undergraduate courses, as students transition to college and begin thinking about their activism and about making change on their campuses.

Overview of Book

Throughout this text, we intentionally center the voices and experiences of identity-based student activists, especially those who possess one or more minoritized identities. In Part I of the book, we provide historical and contextual foundations for the rest of the text. In Chapter 1, we share our personal journeys to this work, highlighting the ways our own experiences and perspectives inform our interpretation of student activists' stories and experiences. Additionally, we provide an overview of the power-conscious framework and critical narrative inquiry to situate our study. Finally, we share information about the participants in our study and our strategies for collecting data. Chapter 2 provides an overview of the historical and current contexts in which student activism has emerged. We situate our study in identity- and power-conscious frameworks, requiring us to examine the history of identity-based movements on college campuses throughout U.S. history. In Chapter 3, we provide additional context for the findings of our study by examining a number of conceptual and theoretical frameworks that may contribute to a deeper understanding of the additional ideas presented in the text. Specifically, we examine concepts of identity and power, emotional labor and racial battle fatigue, institutional betrayal, and neoliberalism as they relate to identity-based student activism. Part I of this text provides a comprehensive foundation for examining identity-based student activism from a critical lens.

In Part II of the text, we illuminate findings from our national study about identity-based student activism. We illuminate identity-based student activists' motivations and strategies for engaging in activism in Chapter 4. Specifically, we examine how students' identities informed their activism and examined the wisdom student activists cultivated as result of their activism. Chapter 5 illuminates the ways identity-based student activism serves as a form of labor, benefitting institutions of higher education. Students engaged in identity-based student activism frequently contribute to the overall improvement of campus climates through their work raising awareness about injustices on campus and demanding improvements to campus practices, often at the expense of their own well-being. In Chapter, 6, we highlight the experiences of educators whom student activists identified as supportive of their work. Educators' stories highlight the complex and contradictory messages they receive from institutional leaders and their strategies for supporting student activists. Finally, in Chapter 7, we provide recommendations for educators who work in identity-based centers, educators and administrators in areas beyond identity-based centers, and faculty for more effectively supporting identity-based student activists. Specifically, we call on educators to step up to do the work of creating equitable campus environments, rather than relying on the unpaid labor of student activists. Further, we implore educators to engage in self-work as a strategy to better understand themselves and their assumptions as they work alongside student activists to improve their climates.

Conclusion

Ultimately, the seven chapters in this book blend together history and power to underscore the ways identity-based activists work to address oppression within their institutions. Centering identity and power illustrates how both concepts provide a more nuanced and complex understanding of student activism. We invite readers to reflect on their own identities throughout this book, as well as their particular contexts, and how both shape their work with activists on their campuses. We now turn to Part I of this book, where we highlight key historical and conceptual information that frames the remaining chapters.

References

Astin, A. W., Astin, H. S., Bayer, A. E., & Bisconti, A. S. (1975). *The power of protest.* San Francisco, CA: Jossey-Bass.

Geiger, R. L. (2016). The ten generations of American higher education. In M. N. Bastedo, P. G. Altbach, & P. J. Gumport (Eds.), *American higher education in the twenty-first century* (4th ed., pp. 3–34). Baltimore, MD: The Johns Hopkins University Press.

Horowitz, H. L. (1987). *Campus life: Undergraduate cultures for the end of the eighteenth century to the present.* New York, NY: Alfred A. Knopf.

Lorde, A. (1984). The master's tools will never dismantle the master's house. In *Sister outsider: Essays and speeches by Audre Lorde.* New York, NY: Ten Speed Press.

Rudolph, F. (1990). *The American college and university: A history.* Athens, GA: University of Georgia Press.

Thelin, J. R. (2011). *A history of American higher education* (2nd ed.). Baltimore, MD: The Johns Hopkins University Press.

ACKNOWLEDGEMENTS

Dear Student Activists,

We see you. We see the labor in which you engage. We see how tirelessly you work to hold your institutions accountable for the values around equity and inclusion they espouse. We see how your institutions benefit from this labor. We see how your mere existence is often a form of activism. We see the oppression and trauma you continuously navigate. We see that you don't have the privilege of just being students.

Although it might seem that you are often isolated in your activism, we want you to know that some faculty, educators, and administrators on your campuses want to be supportive of your work and to do their parts in making campuses a better place. Our hope is that this book offers a roadmap for our colleagues—other educators—so that they can see ways they can be more explicitly supportive and helpful to you in your activism.

We encourage you to use intersectional and multidimensional lenses for your activism. Every person has various social identities that come together to make them who they are. Dominant identities—those identities in which we experience privilege—are the identities we often don't think about because we usually don't have to. This is what we mean by using a multidimensional lens—thinking about your race, class, gender, sexual orientation, and ability, for example, and how they work together to make you who you are (Ferguson, 2019). Intersectionality, however, requires also looking at how different systems of domination work together to create oppression (Crenshaw, 1989; Harris & Patton, 2018). For example, how do racism and sexism manifest simultaneously to make the experiences of Women of Color different than those of white men? Why, for example, might administrators listen more effectively to white men who are activists than to transgender Women of Color activists? Because of how the system of white dominance works, whiteness is positioned as natural and normal, meaning those who are white (or closer to whiteness) are seen as more desirable, and thus, worthy of hearing.

When we think and work in intersectional ways, we understand how different systems work in combination to impact individual people's experiences. For example, activists engaged in the movement for Black Lives and activists engaged around issues of sexual violence may recognize common ways in which current criminal justice systems cause harm to minoritized people. Because police constantly surveil Black and Brown people, Black and Brown people frequently fear physical harm or death at the hands of police officers. Similarly Women of Color experience high rates of police violence in the form of sexual assault committed by police (Ritchie, 2017). Additionally, when survivors of sexual violence report their experiences to police, police often resist them, and they rarely receive any form of justice for the harm perpetrators caused them. Since the current criminal justice system is not working for anyone, what if these activists came together and developed an alternative accountability system that more equitably served people in minoritized communities?

Oppression often pits people with minoritized identities against each other, clamoring for some semblance of power (Linder, 2018). Because of how power works in this way on your campuses, we encourage you to work in solidarity with other activists and not just stick to your single issue. You cannot expend all of your energy trying to combat every oppression; this is why we recommend that you work alongside other activists. For example, if you are a proponent of the movement for Black Lives, your activism within this movement is strengthened by thinking of how Black women are often not centered in the movement or by being inclusive of disabled Black people or transgender Black people. The more you build coalitions across differences, the stronger, more nuanced, and more sustainable your activism will be.

We also know some of you may not identify with the word *activist*. Some of you are simply working to address oppression and trauma because you do not have a choice or see no other way to live than to engage in this work. You are doing it to take care of your communities and to help the people you care about be able to survive on their campuses. You might also actively resist the term *activist* because you see it as something white people or other people with more privileged identities claim. And some of you might not even desire to use any labels because none of them resonate with you. We want you to know that not identifying with this term is okay. You are in good company, as many of the activists in our study did not resonate with this term either. Some of the students preferred to describe their activism as *resistance* or focus on what they are doing without needing to label it. No matter what term you use or do not use, we see the work you are doing and know it matters.

Finally, take care of yourselves. You matter enough to prioritize your own needs. If you need to step aside for some time, give yourself grace and do not punish yourself for needing to do so. Activists who have more dominant identities, step in so those with more minoritized identities can take better care of their needs.

In solidarity,

Chris, Stephen, Alex, Meg, and TJ

References

Crenshaw, K. (1989). Demarginalizing the intersection of race and sex: A black feminist critique of antidiscrimination doctrine, feminist theory and antiracist politics. *University of Chicago Legal Forum, 1*, 139–167.

Ferguson, R. A. (2019). *One-dimensional queer*. Medford, MA: Polity Press.

Harris, J. C., & Patton, L. D. (2018). Un/Doing intersectionality through higher education research. *The Journal of Higher Education*. Advance online publication. doi:10.1080/00221546.2018.1536936

Linder, C. (2018). *Sexual violence on campus: Power-conscious approaches to awareness, prevention, and response*. Bingley, UK: Emerald Publishing Limited.

Ritchie, A. (2017). *Invisible no more: Police violence against black women and women of color*. Boston, MA: Beacon Press.

PART I

Setting the Stage

Foundations, History, and Contexts

Identity

Piecing together the pieces of me
Like a puzzle with no edges
Trying to find the whole me
And yet
As I search, the light gets dimmer
So I resist the piecing together
And embrace the intersections
Not akin to an equation needing to be solved

Power

What happens
When you pay attention?
How does it feel?
Like the first crisp winter day
That send chills down your spine
Like seeing parked vehicles
Enveloped with the first spring pollen
Like the autumn leaves
Hues of bright and muted oranges and reds
When you stop
You notice the things you stopped noticing
Power works in this way
You see it when it's never been yours

You feel it engulf those around you
You seek its presence
Wishing you had an inkling of it
But, also not
For you see the way it bruises
How it crushes everything around you
How it takes without giving
How unforgiving it is
How it cheats life

1

INTRODUCTION

Although student activism is not a new phenomenon (Ferguson, 2017; Rhoads, 1997), a recent resurgence in public, visible activism across college and university campuses has resulted in renewed attention to student activism in scholarship and popular media (Campbell, 2016; Linder, Myers, Riggle, & Lacy, 2016; Lowery, 2017). Many student activists organize to hold their institutions accountable for the oppression perpetuated on college and university campuses; students organize to address racism, classism, homophobia, transphobia, ableism, and sexism, to name a few. Identity-based student activists seldom separate their experiences on campus from issues impacting them in the larger community. They do not have the luxury of "just being a student" (Linder et al., 2019, p. 37); instead, they must address issues of inequity on their campuses while navigating going to classes, working, and participating in co-curricular activities.

Combining findings of a national study on student activism and the authors' experiences working in higher education, we provide insight for student activists, educators, and administrators about the role of power and dominance in campus-based student activism. We use a critical, power-conscious lens to problematize dominant narratives about student activism, including the notion that activists cause trouble, and highlight ways students engaged in identity-based activism contribute to improving campus climates through their labor. Further, we interrogate labels and traditional notions of what constitutes activism as a strategy to validate and support current student activists. Finally, we share strategies for educators, administrators, and faculty to engage more effectively with and learn from student activists on their campuses.

In this chapter, we provide an overview of the language and terminology we use throughout the book, followed by our researcher perspectives and an overview of the theoretical framework that guides our work. We also share the context for our study, including how we collected data and information about the participants of the study.

Language and Terminology

Language constantly evolves, requiring researchers to clearly and explicitly define and describe specific terms on which they rely in their writing. In this book, we use several terms that have multiple meanings, depending on context, so here we describe how we use these specific terms.

Identity-Based Activism

Identity-based activism is organizing, resisting, and engaging with issues directly tied to oppression and identity. Although some students may engage around issues in which they do not experience oppression (e.g., some white people may engage in racial justice activism), many activists engage in resistance related to an identity in which they experience systemic oppression.

Identity-Based Centers

Identity-based centers are spaces on campus that center the experiences of students with a particular identity or set of identities, including women's centers; lesbian, gay, bisexual, and transgender (LGBT) centers; cultural centers; and similar organizations and offices. Although identity-based centers may provide programming focused on a particular identity, generally these centers do not exclude other people; rather, they seek to engage all people to improve the campus climate for minoritized students. Additionally, many identity-based centers intentionally address intersectionality, or the ways that systems of oppression interact to influence people's experiences at the core of more than one minoritized identity.

Dominant Identities

Dominant identities refer to the identities in which a person experiences privilege, or systemic access to resources and experiences that people without that identity may not experience. Other words that people may use to describe dominant identity include agent or privileged identities (Adams et al., 2013). For example, white people have access to racial privilege, cisgender men have access to gender privilege, and people without disabilities have access to ability privilege.

Minoritized Identities

Minoritized identities refer to the identities in which a person experiences systemic oppression or marginalization. In some instances, people may refer to these identities as target or marginalized identities (Adams et al., 2013). We intentionally use minoritized rather than minority to indicate that people with power enact oppression on other people; oppression does not happen with no actors to enact it (Smith, 2016). Examples of minoritized identities include women, transgender people, People of Color, and people with disabilities.

Power

In this text, we use the word power to refer to the ability to influence or significantly alter one's own life or the life of others. Power may be formal or informal. Formal power refers to power one has access to by way of a position in an organizational structure (e.g., a faculty member has power over a student); informal power refers to power one has by way of identity or other non-organizationally related structures (e.g., a man has informal power over a woman in dominant U.S. culture).

Faculty, Staff, Administrators, and Educators

Researchers use a variety of terms to describe the various roles that non-students play on college and university campuses. Some scholars use the language of faculty and staff (Kezar, 2010), while others use *institutional agents* (Bensimon, 2007; Museus & Neville, 2012) to describe people whose roles involve supporting students on campus. Although most scholars do not explicitly define *faculty* or *administrators*, *faculty* frequently includes people who are employed by the institution primarily as classroom instructors and researchers and *administrators* include "any non-faculty member who held power within the university to enable student activists to accomplish their goals or to prevent them from doing so" (Ropers-Huilman, Carwile, & Barnett, 2005, p. 299). The term *staff* is less clear, as it refers to anyone who is not faculty or an administrator, but sometimes also includes administrators. This includes custodial staff, people who work in entry-level positions in student services offices, mid-level managers, and a number of other positions. In this study, we use the term *educators* to describe the people who engage in supporting student activists to highlight the ways that people across the institution work to support students' education. We did not distinguish between faculty, staff, and administrators as we collected data for this study, although we do discuss the ways educators' positionality, including their role at the institution, influences their relationship to student activism.

Study Context and Researcher Positionalities

A number of events converged to bring this work to the forefront of our lives at this time. An increase in attention to police murders of Black and Brown bodies, increased awareness about sexual violence, and an ongoing struggle for the recognition of all of us as our full, complex selves brought us together to embark on this work. Each of us has engaged in some level with activism and resistance throughout our lives and careers, and the renewed attention to student activism brought us together for this project. In fall 2015, as Chris and Stephen observed the uptick in visible, public student activism around issues of racism and sexual violence on college and university campuses, we began to discuss developing a national study to examine the relationships between student activists and administrators on college campuses. Specifically, we wanted to know how students engaged in activism related to identity and oppression experienced their campus administrations and what influenced ways administrators engaged with student activists. Reading national news stories during this time led us to believe that some administrators engaged with activists as collaborators and change makers, while others resisted student activism as it related to addressing climate issues on their campuses. To explore these questions, we invited some graduate students and colleagues working in identity-based centers on college and university campuses to engage in a comprehensive study on identity-based student activism. Different from many previous studies on student activism, we sought to intentionally and explicitly examine identity and power in student activism.

In fall 2016, we convened a research team consisting of nine graduate students and two full-time student affairs educators. We discussed our collective interests in this topic and developed strategies for collecting data. We collected and read newspaper articles about student activism to help inform our process. We also read previous scholarship about student activism in the higher education literature. Fall 2016 also resulted in one of the most contentious and divisive presidential campaigns in recent U.S. history. The political climate, including the election of Donald J. Trump as president of the United States, illustrated the level of overt hate and bigotry that fueled many of the movements that students organized around prior to the election. Although many so-called progressive or liberal people credit the 2016 election as another turning point for identity-based activism throughout the United States, many minoritized people knew the level of hatred that existed in the world and were not the least bit surprised by the election results. In fact, they/we had been organizing long before the hate-filled election based on their/our knowledge, understanding, and experiences of hate and harm prior to November 2016. The election was a *result* of the hatred and bigotry, not the impetus for it. We explore the specific contexts in which these movements occurred more in Chapter 2.

The research team ebbed and flowed over the course of the study. Members' roles included helping with participant recruitment, conducting interviews, managing and organizing data, analyzing data, and discussing findings as they emerged. Although the process of using a research team is messy and logistically challenging, we believe in this case the number of people involved at various stages of the process resulted in deeper thinking about student activism because of the integration of multiple perspectives and experiences. We regularly met to discuss the process, which resulted in us being able to think as we worked, rather than waiting until the end to analyze the data. Although multiple people participated in the research process over time, five of us came together to write this book. Specifically, the five of us authored this text because of our collective experience working with student activists throughout our careers.

Researcher Positionalities

Each of the authors of this book brings a unique positionality related to student activism, and our perspectives inform our approach to scholarship and practice in higher education. Specifically, four of the five of us have worked in identity-based centers on a variety of college and university campuses, contributing to an in-depth understanding of the ways college students experience identity-based oppression, including racism, sexism, homophobia, and transphobia. Additionally, all of us have engaged in multiple research projects about campus activism, examining the ways that identity and power influence student activists' experiences on campus, faculty experiences as scholar-activists, the roles of educators engaged in identity-based advocacy, and the use of social media as a site for identity-based activism. The work of understanding ourselves and the ways our socialization influences our experiences in the world never ends, yet pausing to reflect and articulate our understanding of our own socialization helps use to make conscious our assumptions, values, and beliefs about how we see the world and how those in the world see us. Below, we share parts of our journeys that led us to collaborating on this research project.

Chris

I am a queer, cisgender, white, educated woman raised in a working-class family. I am non-disabled and do not identify with any religion, though I grew up celebrating Christian holidays and am familiar with Christian traditions. These are my salient identities, those that are important to me and inform how I see the world. Additionally, I am a faculty member in a higher education graduate program and have been full-time faculty for the past eight years. Prior to becoming faculty, I worked in student affairs for 10 years, spending the bulk of my career as the director of a campus-based women's center, where I advocated for survivors of interpersonal violence and provided education about interpersonal violence for faculty, staff, and students on campus. Although faculty and peers exposed me to issues of equity and inclusion in my master's program, working in a campus-based women's center pushed me to have my own racial awakening and develop a deeper understanding of the ways all forms of oppression are connected. As a cisgender white woman, I spent the early part of my student affairs career coming to understand how patriarchy and sexism had impacted my life, including as a secondary survivor of domestic violence. I grew up in a home where violence occurred, but did not understand the depth of how it impacted me until my mid-twenties. As the director of a campus-based women's center, I quickly learned that my experience with patriarchy and sexism was both similar and different from the people around me. Specifically, I started to understand that my experiences as a white woman situated me differently than my Women of Color colleagues. I began to learn the harmful ways white women had ignored and minimized the unique experiences of Women of Color around issues of interpersonal violence, causing significant pain to Women of Color and failing to adequately address issues of interpersonal violence.

My new-to-me understanding of racism in feminist organizing led me to continually reflecting on the role of race and racism in my life and to interrogating ways I had perpetuated racism in feminist organizing. I devoured intersectional feminist anthologies, including *The Color of Violence* (Incite, 2006), and participated in as many trainings and workshops as I could to better understand my role in interrupting white dominance in feminist organizing. Additionally, I did my best to interrupt structural power and dominance in the student affairs unit I coordinated and hired the most diverse staff that I could, resulting in some of the most powerful growth in my career. Genderqueer students taught me that "women"-centered programming did not always feel welcoming to them; Students of Color taught me that failing to intentionally center race in our work would result in continued focus on white women's experiences. Survivors with disabilities taught me that the systems set up to address issues of violence frequently failed to consider the relationship between mental illness and violence. In the women's center, we intentionally tried to create space for students on the margins of the margins—those who were not welcomed in other spaces on campus—to find a home with us. This was my first experience supporting student activists. I learned to create space, then to either get out of the way or to sit and listen. I learned to leverage the power I had within the institution to center minoritized students' experiences when they wanted me to, and when they did not, to validate their experiences with pain and marginalization. I learned that sometimes just having a community to practice vulnerability and growth, push back and be heard, celebrate successes, and learn from each other was the most powerful form of support I could provide.

These experiences led me to my first research project—exploring the experiences of undergraduate Women of Color activists. I had read about the experiences of Women of Color in feminist organizing in previous generations and I wanted to know if the same challenges still existed. Of course, they do. I interviewed seven undergraduate Women of Color engaged in feminism and learned that most of them did not resonate with the label of "activist"; they saw their roles in activism as a strategy for survival and a responsibility and even sometimes a burden that students around them were not carrying. A decade later, Students of Color across the country are telling us the same thing—their existence on college and university campuses is a form of resistance and activism.

Since then, I have continued to examine student activism in a number of ways, including exploring white feminist women's understanding of their whiteness in feminism, the strategies of activists engaged in addressing campus sexual violence, and the influence of power on identity-based campus activists' experiences. Although my experience in a campus-based women's center continues to be the most profound learning experience of my career, these research projects help me to continue to understand the ways oppression impacts students and my role in continuing to interrupt power and dominance in my circles of influence, which admittedly grow larger and larger the longer I am in higher education.

Stephen

I am a Black/Ghanaian, cisgender, educated man who is from a middle-class background. I also identify strongly as an immigrant. The slash between "Black" and "Ghanaian" means at times I feel more like a Black American, given my socialization in the United States; at other moments, I feel more Ghanaian. When I am surrounded by my family eating rice and peanut butter soup, plantains, and fufu, my immigrant identity is very salient. I have only come to recently explore my cisgender male privilege, often through hard conversations with women in my life, specifically my former partner. This experience, in particular, has given me more empathy for white people engaged in examining their white dominance.

I have also been a faculty member for 11 years now, and these experiences have informed my passion for activism. Early on as a faculty member at the University of Maryland, I noticed the ways the promotion and tenure system devalued the service in which most women and Faculty of Color engaged. I spoke out vehemently about this at every opportunity I was afforded during faculty meetings. I, however, never considered myself an activist.

On August 9, 2014, Darren Wilson shot and killed Michael Brown, a Black teenager, in Ferguson, Missouri. I saw images of Michael Brown's lifeless body tweeted and retweeted on social media. I felt numb and angry simultaneously. This all occurred six days before I was to submit my promotion and tenure materials at Miami University. I remember feeling like tenure did not matter when I felt too afraid in my Black body. I also had a palpable fear for my multiracial son's life. To make sense of my pain, I connected with two former colleagues at Miami, one of whom grew up a few miles from Ferguson. We began talking and listening to each other. We did not want Michael Brown's death to be in vain. So, we formed what we called the Mobilizing Anger Collective to bring faculty, students, and community members together to address injustices on Miami's campus and the surrounding Oxford, Ohio, environment. From these experiences, I started to embrace my identity as an activist, more specifically, a scholar-activist, who blended my research, teaching, and service with my own activism. The Mobilizing Anger Collective helped me not feel so alone and provided me with friends and colleagues with whom to engage in activism.

In my work on activism, I have connected with a number of master's students who are trying to figure out how to balance their roles as students, activists, and campus employees, often receiving mixed messages from supervisors about the extent to which they are "allowed" to engage in activism alongside undergraduate students. These experiences have deepened my desire to understand activists engaged in identity-based activism and how administrators create circumstances that make it difficult for activists to work to improve their campuses. These experiences translated into a class I taught during the spring 2019 semester about activism to help graduate students make sense of their own activism and learn how to support activists.

As someone who holds many dominant identities (sexual orientation, class, education, gender, ability), I have benefited from the many stories of activists, and my interest in this book is to center the stories of these activists so that those with dominant identities might use their power to enable minoritized activists to live more freely in their bodies.

Alex

I was born and raised in South Florida. More specifically, in Plantation, Florida, a suburb of Fort Lauderdale. Uttering the name of my hometown always makes me uneasy. Growing up in South Florida gave me a different picture of the United States than most people experience. I had more diverse experiences in schooling than many from even only an hour north of me. Race was also never a binary of Black or white. While I did not realize it until later in life, having extended families of two different worlds and experiences helped shape many of my views on the world, on empathy, and on justice. While my father's family is predominantly white and of German descent, my mother's family is more mixed, with lineage from Jamaica, East India, and Chile. My mother is the lightest skinned of her siblings, though all three could pass as white in certain contexts. More recently, in similar but distinct ways from Stephen, I have identified as both white/multiracial, knowing that I am often rendered and recognized as white and benefit from whiteness. At the same time, the early influences my mother's family had on me, particularly the years of being raised by my aunt, contributed to my socialization in unique ways that always make me feel out of place in majority or all-white spaces. In many ways, I long to be back in South Florida, to be back in an enclave that makes me feel at home.

My first witnessing of postsecondary student activism was actually from a distance. In February 2013, the Florida Atlantic University (FAU) Foundation, my alma mater, accepted a multimillion dollar gift from the GEO Group, one of the nation's largest private prison groups. The founder, George Zoley, is an FAU alumnus. In return, the GEO Group gained the naming rights to the university's new and first football stadium. Students, faculty members, and alumni were (rightfully) outraged. The GEO Group had multiple, documented human rights abuses charged against it. In response, students organized campaigns to embarrass the university and compel them to return the gift; Stephen Colbert even discussed the issue on his Comedy Central show *The Colbert Report*. While I was at the

University of Georgia at the time, I was connected via social media with the various constituencies leading the charge. The power of activism became clear to me when, in April, the GEO Group withdrew its gift from the university because of the continued, unyielding pressure from students and faculty.

The summer of 2013 was pivotal for me. At the time, I served as a graduate summer intern at Loyola University Chicago for a program designed to help rising junior and senior high school students experience college via a credit-bearing course and living on campus. Working with a great staff in one of my favorite cities reminded me why I loved working in higher education and making a difference in students' lives. That summer was full of national events that both excited and activated me. First, that June, the U.S. Supreme Court declared Section 3 of the Defense of Marriage Act unconstitutional in *U.S. v Windsor*. Possibility for myself as a queer person and my community had opened up in a way that was previously unavailable to us. However, a month later, I still remember in vivid detail sitting in the common room of the ground floor of Messina Hall. It was cold, and the majority of the students in the program were out on a trip. My supervisor, one of our undergraduate staff members, and I were discussing something when news of George Zimmerman's not guilty verdict popped up in my Facebook feed. The news shook me to my core. I was enraged and desolate. How could something so obvious, so blatant as the murder of Trayvon Martin be seen as anything but continued racist violence? How could Zimmerman possibly be rendered innocent when all signs pointed to his guilt? As the summer came to an end, I came back to my graduate program at the University of Georgia hungry to figure out how I could position my student affairs praxis in such a way to uplift and support the work of student activists who pushed back, disrupted, and challenged their institutions and communities to be better.

Assuming my role as assistant director of the Lesbian, Gay, Bisexual, and Transgender Resource Center at Michigan State University allowed me an outlet to further the work I felt was so necessary and pivotal. I advised the LGBTQ student organization, which represented the community officially on campus and forged relationships with leaders in the Council of Racial and Ethnic Students, especially the Black Student Alliance. On the evening of Monday, November 24, as I was frantically packing for an early flight back home to be with my family for the first time since moving to Michigan, the news of Darren Wilson's non-indictment came through my social media feeds. Communicating with student leaders and activists that night, I quickly finished packing and headed to campus for several hours, into the early hours of the morning. The Black Student Alliance had organized the gathering within hours; over 150 people showed up. Students spoke of loving on one another harder and pushing back even harder. Exhausted and spent, the ensuing days showed me the labor student activists undertake to address issues of injustice and inequity.

In February 2017, my foray into the study of student activism formally began with an invitation from Chris to join the #ActivismOnCampus team. At the same time the team collected the narrative data from the student activists and supportive educators we share later in the book, we also discussed philosophies of activism, our own experiences supporting students, and how we could leverage our project to more directly support the activists themselves. These conversations and learnings have continued to inform my own work, particularly as I approach my dissertation and think more about the conditions of anti-racist solidarity, both what promotes it and what hinders it.

Meg

I'm most often described as colorful leaning towards crass, with a quick wit and amicable energy. But what I'd like to be best known for is a deep sense of thoughtfulness and care. While I pride myself on centering love in all I do, my whiteness has placed a veil over me for years, leaving me void of love, care, or even thought about many of those around me. Let me explain.

I'm white. Like white white. Like Irish, English, and Hungarian white. Like "freckled, green eyes, auburn hair" white. Like "growing up in an all-white suburb of Chicago" white. Like "spending my childhood through adolescence at a 98% white megachurch" white. Like "not knowing I was white till I was in college" white. Like "knowing I was queer before I knowing I was white" white. Yeah, that white. And like all privileges that come with our dominant identities, I have had—and still have—a lot to unlearn. Whiteness is endemic, endless, and so deeply normalized as what's right and good that it has rendered me thoughtless at times and unable to genuinely love those around me. I am ashamed and mournful of the pain I have caused, do cause, and will cause People of Color, especially Black folks, in my life. I'm ashamed of the ways that I have failed to show up and show out for Students of Color, including many student activists, throughout my career. I'm ashamed by my lack of thoughtfulness, but glad that I can now (often, not always) name and interrupt my white dominance, fragility, and privilege when it shows up. While I am just (relatively speaking) learning about my white identity, how it shows up, how it is seen, how it gives me access to more than I might ever know, and how I can begin to unlearn the false confidence it has given me, I have spent the majority of my life reconciling my queer and trans identity.

I love queer people. I love trans people. I love our ability to resist, recreate, redesign, reimagine, and rely on each other. I love our ability to create our own world, our own rules, and to exemplify love in what we do. But I haven't always. Though I have known I was queer in both sexuality and gender, I pushed it away, hid it (not well), and was deeply ashamed of who I was and who I loved. My hatred of self manifested in multiple ways, leading to a long and sordid undergraduate collegiate career. In and out of multiple colleges for 10 years, I learned a lot about both myself and the necessity for student support that is holistic and authentic. Like many of us, central to my praxis, I strive to be who I desperately needed when I was younger.

I most recently served as the director of the LGBT resource center at the University of Georgia. Before working at UGA, I did queer and trans student support work at Carnegie Mellon University. I have spent the last decade of my life dedicating myself to student support, advocacy, and care, particularly as it pertains to queer and trans students. However, I think I have only been doing it well for the last handful of years. I say this not in a self-deprecating sort of way. It has only been in the last handful of years that I have gotten endless, painful, and exhausting pushback on my advocacy for and with students and student activists. This pushback coincides with a change in how I approached my work. Thanks in large part to some amazing queer and trans students, this #ActivismOnCampus research team, and faculty and colleagues on my doctoral journey, I have changed how I approach everything in my life, including my student affairs praxis. I approach the work from a place that centers and honors the experiences of students in the margins, often those who hold multiple minoritized identities, because I believe that if we serve these students well, we serve all others along the way.

I would also be remiss if I did not credit my wife for my continued growth and development as it pertains to my dominant identities. She is eager to call me out, in, around, and above in a graceful and kind way that allows me to take ownership for my actions regardless of my intent. And finally, I believe in the power of student activists to change campuses, our nation, and the world. I believe they are a large part of what make higher education powerful and meaningful. At one year old, one of my son's favorite books is *A is for Activist*, and I hope in 2036, he will be engaged in student activism too.

TJ

I am a Black, fat-bodied, queer, cisgender man who comes from a single-parent, low-income home in Columbus, Ohio. Most importantly, I was raised by women, and from an early age I was taught to center a radical Black feminist politic in my life to inform how I understood the world. Growing up in a poor, primarily Black neighborhood situated for me the realities of power and dominance, and my immediate environment would come to inform how I navigated oppressive systems, structures, and secure my survival in the world.

When I finally attended college, it was a shock to my system. Not because I was unprepared academically; in fact, I did well in coursework. The shock came from being in an educational environment where the majority of people around me did not "look like me." The corresponding microaggressions and violence of being in a space dominated by whiteness lit a fire in my core, and as result I became a student activist on campus, engaging in marches, protests, and other demonstrative acts to highlight and disrupt the ways Black students were experiencing racism. In addition to this, I found myself avoiding student leadership opportunities or experiences that were not rooted or centered in support of and by Black students, despite the prevalence of requests I received to be involved in more general student leadership organizations and opportunities.

During my undergraduate career, I had the opportunity to work in our campus multicultural center as a work-study student. It was a formative experience that provided me with language to articulate the experiences I was having with power and dominance, however, that experience also provided new and more nuanced understandings of power, specifically anti-Blackness. It was during that time I learned that even people with minoritized identities (including non-Black People of Color) can approximate themselves close to power and dominance and be rewarded for oppressing others. During this time, I also wrestled with and came to new understandings regarding how my experiences with oppression (in my minoritized identities) did not render invisible my realities with my privileged identities (cisgender man, able-bodied, etc.). Those realizations birthed in me a more meaningful ethic around coalition-building and advocacy for others, their issues and concerns, which in turn manifested as community-organizing and creating connections between the university and the Columbus community.

I worked with the multicultural center for approximately eight years (off and on) as a work-study student, graduate administrative associate, interim program coordinator, and finally assistant director. As I reflect back, what is fascinating about my transitions is that, in many ways, student affairs administrators (who ultimately became my colleagues when I pursued the same career) and institutional leaders engaged in a sort of revisionist account of who I was and how I resisted oppressive structures as a student. I began to be remembered as a "student affairs golden child" and not the disruptor that I was—and am. My ability to navigate white supremacist spaces, to code-switch, to undermine was almost undetected because of my academic and extracurricular success. I was almost viewed as "transcending" my Blackness in the view of my new colleagues.

As I transitioned from undergraduate student to graduate student to full-time staff, my relationships to and with activism on campus shifted dramatically. Further, in addition to my responsibilities in the center, I also had roles connected to our campus bias assessment group and a campus campaign related to addressing acts of hate/bias through responsive programming. While it seemed I was positioned to be especially supportive of minoritized students and student activists, the expectation of my role (at times) seemed to be more about surveilling college student activists and their movements, and managing them on behalf of the institution. I was left with the difficult situation of determining how to navigate the minefield of being an institutional agent while not abandoning my values of equity and justice. As such, I began to resist by undermining, in various ways, the problematic directives from university administration as a means to support student activists more meaningfully, at some risk to my own career and livelihood.

As a staff member I had the opportunity to witness college student activists during the height of the George Zimmerman trial, solidarity events during #ConcernedStudent1950, and organizing by a vibrant community of women who advocated for institutional support for women student services on campus.

Through these and other campus demonstrations, I became interested in how each of these phenomena (student activists and their experiences with oppression, educators in identity-centers and their support of student activists, and institutional responses to college student activist) were working together and their implications.

When I began doctoral studies, I had the opportunity to join the #ActivismOnCampus research team, which led to this study and, consequently, this text. This experience has been incredible; it not only provided me opportunities to engage with college student activists and the educators who support them, but also has given me ideas for how to support activists and educators as we work collectively to undermine, to disrupt, to liberate.

Our collective experiences and reflections inform how we engage with the research and each other through this research project. During the data collection and analyses processes and the subsequent discussion and writing of this book and other articles, we have challenged, supported, and pushed each other to be better, more conscious versions of ourselves as activists, educators, and scholars.

Power-Conscious Framework

In this study, we employed a power-conscious framework to examine the relationships among student activists, educators who support them, and the institutions at which they exist. The power-conscious framework builds on critical consciousness and intersectionality to challenge scholars, educators, and activists to maintain a constant awareness of power and its role in all of our interactions. As Chris highlights elsewhere:

> Systems of oppression operate by maintaining the status quo, by attempting to make people believe that if they work hard enough, that if they change themselves enough, they too, can be successful in current systems. A power-conscious framework challenges scholars and activists to re-consider current structures and to consider ways for dismantling and restructuring systems to share power, rather than building structures that contribute to one group having power over another group.
>
> Activists and educators frequently focus on the needs of minoritized communities and people who are harmed by oppression, and rightfully so. Focusing on the needs of and listening to minoritized people is essential for dismantling systems of oppression. However, oppressors maintain systems of oppression by busy-ing people, especially minoritized people, with focusing on addressing the symptoms and outcomes of oppression, rather than addressing oppression at its roots. If oppressors can keep oppressed people busy and preoccupied with taking care of each other and attempting to break into the structures that currently exist, then oppressors do not have to change their behavior or the systems that benefit them.
>
> *(Linder, 2018, p. 19)*

Defining Power

Although critical scholars rarely use a common definition of power, they do recognize and critique systematic domination and subordination of People of Color, queer people, women, poor people, disabled people, and other minoritized groups (Adams et al., 2013; Johnson, 2006; Tatum, 2000). In our work, we share these critiques and define power using two constructs: social constructions and power over versus power with. Additionally, we recognize the relationship between formal and informal power.

The concept of social construction and power explains the ways that identities have come to mean things over time in mainstream U.S. culture. Scholars frequently define social identity as a social construction, meaning that people with power have historically created meaning for identity over time (Johnson, 2006; Takaki, 2008). For example, although the social construction of race has little biological support, white people in the United States have defined racial categories, determining who is considered white and who has access to white privilege. When Irish people first immigrated to the United States, they were not considered white; however, when white people realized that they needed more numbers to retain the majority in politics and other powerful realms, they decided to classify Irish people as white (Takaki, 2008). Gender, sexual orientation, ability, and other identities have similar social constructions—people with power have given meaning to these various identities. The complexity of this issue, however, is that people with minoritized identities have also given identities meaning over time. Because people with power oppress minoritized people, many groups of minoritized people have reclaimed their identities, working to give the identities their own meaning. For example, historically, people with power used the term queer as a negative descriptor of LGBT people; however, today, some queer people have reclaimed the word queer as an attempt to take power back from those with formal power and to redefine the term in their own ways (Warner, 1999).

The second concept related to power is the difference between *power with* and *power over*. Borrowing from the business management literature, some feminists have described ways people may engage in power with people, rather than power over people (Boje & Rosile, 2001). Power with illustrates the idea that people may engage in shared power relationships. For example, in some radical organizing spaces, members of organizations choose not to elect formal positional leaders to promote a power with process, meaning that all members of the organization share power and responsibility for ensuring the organization runs smoothly (McDowell, 2012). In more hierarchical organizations, like institutions of higher education, some leaders have power over other people in the organization. Most of the time this power is associated with positional leadership, including a variety of titles and positions that include supervisory and other forms of power relationships.

Although the discussion of power with versus power over relies on formal positions of power to maintain power over, positional power is often associated with social identity power, a kind of informal power. Formal power frequently comes in the form of authority gained through position in a hierarchy. Informal power may include influence and authority gained through social constructions and relationships, regardless of positional power. For example, a white person, no matter where they are positioned in an institutional hierarchy has some power in most organizations simply as a result of their racial identity. Formal and informal power also relate to and inform each other; leaders of institutions of higher education are disproportionately white and male (Pritchard & McChesney, 2018), which are also social identities that possess access to power. It is not coincidental that people with access to informal power through their social identities also often possess formal power through leadership positions within organizations. Informal power frequently leads to more formal power.

Finally, Black feminists and womanist scholars have noted the ways power materializes in the lives of minoritized people is multiplicative:

> I [bell hooks] began to use the phrase in my work "white supremacist capitalist patriarchy" because I wanted to have some language that would actually remind us continually of the interlocking systems of domination that define our reality and not to just have one thing be like, you know, gender is the important issue, race is the important issue, but for me the use of that particular jargonistic phrase was a way, a sort of short cut way of saying all of these things actually are functioning simultaneously at all times in our lives.
>
> *(Media Education Foundation, 1997)*

In this way, it is important to recognize that our articulation of power is centered on the reality that power differentially affects individuals based on the social identities they hold. Power is not a single-issue concept. Power is systemic, structural, and connected to systems of oppression and dominance and informed by social identity.

A Power-Conscious Framework

A power-conscious framework requires scholars and activists to address the symptoms *and* the roots of oppression. The framework is action-oriented, requiring people to engage in awareness and action at the same time, rather than waiting to engage in action after knowing enough. Although those of us engaged in social justice work must be thoughtful and intentional in our work to address equity, we can never know enough—we must do something, learn from it, and go back out and act again. We (the authors of this text) used this framework to guide our research design and analysis as well as the way we reflected and wrote this text.

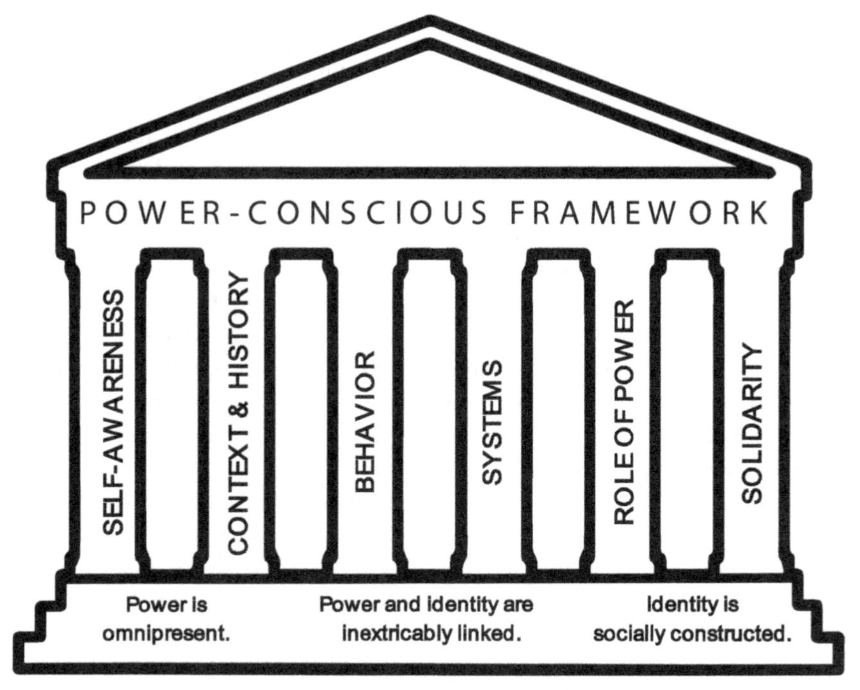

Several assumptions undergird the power-conscious framework: power is present in every interaction between people and between people and systems; power and social identities are inextricably linked; and history matters. Based on these underlying assumptions, the power-conscious framework includes six tenets to guide researchers, activists, and educators in their work. Tenets of a framework provide a way for scholars and activists to interrogate or analyze an idea, phenomenon, policy, or practice to improve them for future use. In this framework, each of the tenets begins with an action word, reminding those using the framework to be actively engaged in doing something with the knowledge, experience, and information they have. Figure 1.1 provides a visual representation of the framework.

The action-oriented tenets of the power-conscious framework include the following: a) engage in critical consciousness and self-awareness; b) consider history and context when examining issues of oppression; c) change behaviors based on reflection and awareness; d) call attention to dominant group members' investment in and benefit from systems of domination; e) interrogate the role of power in individual interactions, policy development, and implementation of practice; and f) work in solidarity to address oppression. We explain each tenet in detail in the sections that follow.

Engage in Critical Consciousness and Self-Awareness

Developing critical consciousness and engaging in self-reflective behaviors provides a starting point for engaging in power-conscious work. People with multiple dominant identities (e.g., white, educated, cisgender, non-disabled people) frequently do not notice the ways people with minoritized identities experience the world; therefore, critical consciousness and self-awareness are especially important in areas in which people experience privilege. Critical consciousness does not mean that people are continually critiquing everything around them; rather, it means that we pay attention to the dynamics in our work spaces and note which people are present and which people are left out of the work. Further, it means that we put ourselves in situations where we can engage in ongoing learning about ourselves and the people around us. One strategy for practicing critical consciousness and self-awareness is to attend programs and events on campus designed to raise awareness about different people's experiences. Make it a goal to attend at least one event on campus each month that centers an identity group to which you do not belong, but make sure that those events are designed for you. Some events are specifically for minoritized people to come together in community as a way to heal from the oppression they experience in the world; other events are designed to educate dominant group members about the experiences of minoritized people. Pay attention and attend the events designed to educate you. Read books and blogs; watch videos and documentaries describing the experiences and realities of people whose experiences are different from your own. Pay attention to what comes up for you in these spaces—what are your takeaways and how is your experience similar and different to what you are hearing?

Although building self-awareness and critical consciousness are certainly work, it is the beginning, not the end, of social justice work. Reflecting for the sake of reflecting without engaging in action perpetuates self-aggrandizement, especially in our dominant identities. Further, although we may feel overwhelmed or immobilized by our understanding of oppression, we must work through these barriers to engage in action, knowing the action will always be imperfect.

Consider History and Context When Examining Issues of Oppression

In addition to developing self-awareness and a critical consciousness in current contexts, we must also pay attention to the ways history and context have influenced the institutionalization of oppression. As Chris describes,

> Ahistoricism, or the failure of people to consider how systems of oppression have been engrained and interwoven into the very fabric of systems, policies, and practices, leads to ineffective strategies for addressing oppression (Delgado & Stefancic, 2012). For example, sexual violence laws in the U.S.

> first emerged as property crime laws. White, owning-class men were the only people who could file sexual violence charges in the 17th and early 18th centuries (Donat & D'Emilio, 1992; Freedman, 2013; Lindemann, 1984). If their wives or daughters were raped or sexually violated, men could claim that their property had been violated. Courts and legal systems did not allow women to own property or have any legal standing, so only men could make a claim related to the sexual violation of women (Freedman, 2013). Although this law has changed, understanding the significance of it in history helps to better explain and address issues of sexism in the legal system today.
>
> *(Linder, 2018, p. 27)*

In addition to historical context, educators and activists must also pay attention to the current contexts in which they work and how those contexts impact people. For example, supporting student activists at a small, religiously affiliated private college is vastly different from supporting student activists at a large, public institution under the microscope of a conservative state legislature. Similarly, student experiences at a Historically Black College or University (HBCU) differ from student experiences at a mid-size regional college. Each context presents its own unique challenges and failing to consider these differences results in ineffective strategies for supporting student activists. Learning the history and context of various campuses and issues student activists strive to address may result in more effective efforts to address oppression. Helping activists understand related movements from the past can help inform their own activism and potentially develop different strategies for working with administrators and other activists.

Change Behaviors Based on Reflection and Awareness

Developing a commitment to self-awareness, critical consciousness, and an awareness of history and context are only the first steps in engaging in a power-conscious framework. Awareness must result in changing behaviors that one knows are harmful. Often referred to as praxis, we must reflect, engage in action, reflect on the action, then act again based on what we learned from our reflection (Freire, 2000/1970; hooks, 1994). When we fail to act because we feel like we do not know enough or because we are overwhelmed, we contribute to continued oppression and harm. Similar to the ways self-awareness is an important first step of critical consciousness, individual-level change is an important first step in systemic change. Although one might sometimes feel as though change at the individual level is not enough, it is something, and because individuals make up systems, individual-level change can result in systemic change. Examples of individual-level change resulting in systemic change include ways we have changed our language related to gender. Individual people have challenged student affairs educators to be more mindful of the ways gender binaries harm students. As a result of individual people speaking up and changing their own language, some systemic-level change has begun to happen. Rather than organizing roommates for social justice retreats based exclusively on participants' sex, some educators have moved toward asking students for roommate preferences, not solely based on sex.

Name and Call Attention to Dominant Group Members' Investment in and Benefit From Systems of Domination

In addition to changing individual-level behaviors, people engaging a power-conscious framework should also work to address systemic-level change. One important strategy for addressing systemic-level change is to call attention to the ways systems disproportionately favor people with dominant identities and to name power as it relates to systems of oppression. One clear example of over-relying on systems that favor people with dominant identities includes most campus responses to hate and bias incidents. Despite the fact that People of Color and queer and trans people experience significant harm and inequity in criminal justice systems, most campus administrators' first response to a hate or bias incident is to ask people harmed by the incident to report the incident to the police. The harmed person then runs the risk of being re-traumatized by engaging with a person or system who may not understand the significance of the harm they experienced.

We (people with dominant identities) frequently maintain our investment in systems that work for us to uphold our comfort and dominance. Although the criminal justice system in its current form arguably does not work well for most of us, we continue to push people who have been harmed to report to the police, rather than exploring alternative mechanisms for healing and accountability because exploring additional strategies requires vulnerability and admitting that we do not know something. It requires people who are used to being in control to let go of some control and listen to people who typically do not have access to formal power. It requires letting go of some privilege to finally create a system that works for more people. Divesting from privilege does not automatically equate to losing power, but it does automatically equate to sharing power, which is often interpreted as losing power. Creating a system of accountability that serves everyone does not necessarily mean that people who are currently served by the system in place will no longer be served; it just means that more people may be served. Calling attention to investment in privilege requires significant shifts in ways of thinking and behaving, including letting go of some of the privileges we are used to, like comfort and familiarity.

Interrogate the Role of Power in Policy and Practice

Paying attention to the ways individual people benefit from and invest in systems of oppression moves us closer to understanding the ways power manifests in policy and practice. Consistently asking the following questions may lead to a deeper awareness of the role of power in policy and practice:

- Who is centered in this program/policy?
- Who is erased or ignored through this program/policy?
- Who does this policy exclude, intentionally or unintentionally? How are power structures developed and sustained in this work?
- What is the impact of power (or lack thereof) on people's real and lived experiences?

For example, when looking at mentoring practices, we can use the power-conscious framework to interrogate how we engage with mentoring as a whole. Bias and power play significant, yet often unnamed, roles in the mentor/mentee relationship. The power-conscious framework helps to uncover and address biases held within our dominant identities along with our participation in structures of oppression in an effort to better serve those we mentor. Utilizing this framework, one question to ask yourself when serving as mentor may be "What are some ways you role model an investment in and benefit from racism/anti-blackness, transphobia, and xenophobia, among other forms of oppression?"

Work in Solidarity to Address Oppression

Exploring the role of power and privilege in individual experiences sometimes results in people with power deciding who gets to do what work. For example, sometimes white people demand that they should be the only people talking to other white people about racism to "protect" People of Color. Similarly, some people argue that only cisgender men should be talking to other cisgender men to address sexism and cissexism so that women and nonbinary people do not have to do the additional labor of educating all of the time. Telling people what they should and should not do based on their identities further contributes to paternalism and ongoing oppression, especially as it relates to minoritized identities.

Working in solidarity with each other to engage in social justice work results in more effective practices. When people with power determine whose role it is to do what work, it is likely that they are passing over people with exceptional talents and skills. Additionally, for some people, working with and educating oppressors is part of their healing process, and gatekeepers should not be responsible for determining who gets to do what.

In conjunction with the power-conscious framework, we used critical narrative methodology to conduct a study about campus activism. By talking with 25 student activists and 17 educators those students identified as "supportive," we sought to understand how student activists and educators thought about their roles in addressing oppressive campus structures and systems.

Critical Narrative Methodology

Using narrative inquiry (Clandinin & Connelly, 2000) and a critical paradigm (Kincheloe & McLaren, 2000), we examined the experiences of students engaged in identity-related activism or resistance on college campuses and the educators who supported them. Narrative inquiry allows researchers to understand people's experiences with a phenomenon through storytelling and counters master narratives about an experience by centering the voices of historically minoritized people (Delgado, 1989). A critical paradigm highlights the role of power in people's experiences (Kincheloe & McLaren, 2000). Specifically, the ontology and epistemology of a critical paradigm require researchers to consider the role of power in knowledge construction and generation. Combining narrative inquiry with a critical paradigm pushes researchers to interrogate the role of power, privilege, and oppression in the research process, including data analysis and interpretation of the findings (Kincheloe & McLaren, 2000).

Data Collection

We recruited participants for this study by asking student affairs educators to share a flyer with students who may meet the criteria for the study. We sought students "engaged in identity-based activism or resistance, 18 years of age or older, and current undergraduate or graduate student (or left your institution in December 2015 or later)." *Identity-related activism or resistance* included any work toward social change related to oppression based on a social identity (e.g., race, class, gender, sexual orientation). Students self-selected into the study, and we did not turn any student away from participating. As part of the interview process, we asked student activists to identify educators who had been supportive of their work as activists, and then we contacted those educators to conduct interviews. Of the 33 educators that students identified, 17 consented to participate in an interview with a member of the research team. We heard back from a handful of educators that they were supportive of the study and glad to have been identified but that they did not feel comfortable participating in the study because they were afraid of the consequences of speaking out about supporting student activism on their campuses. This fear of consequences is telling about the context in which many educators operate. We surmise that some of the additional people who chose not to participate also struggled with some of the same challenges, including fear of speaking out and concerns about their anonymity if they did speak out.

Our research team interviewed 25 student activists and 17 educators over the course of nine months, from October 2016 to May 2017. We used a semi-structured interview protocol, and interviews lasted between 30 and 75 minutes. We conducted the interviews in person, using video-conferencing (Google Hangout,

Skype, or FaceTime), or by telephone. The interview protocol for students included questions like:

- What is your definition of activism? Do you identify with this term or prefer a different term?
- How do your identities influence the kinds of activism you're engaged with?
- What is your relationship with administrators related to your activism?

For educators, questions included:

- Why do you think that a student identified you as supportive of their work?
- What messages do you receive from your supervisor about student activism?
- What strategies do you use to support student activists?

Participants and Setting

Although describing demographics of participants sometimes seems essentializing and reductionistic, we describe the demographics of the participants in this study to provide some context for readers. We do not intend to assume that people with a shared identity have a monolithic experience, yet it is important to acknowledge ways identities intersect with systems of oppression to influence people's experiences with campus-based activism. Compared to the educator participants, we provide some additional detail about the student participants in this study by associating participants' pseudonyms with their identities as a strategy to help the reader more fully understand the relationship between students' identities and experiences. We do not connect educator participants' pseudonyms with their identities to protect their confidentiality. Many educator participants expressed concern about people at their institutions finding out that they participated in the study. They were concerned that they may suffer negative consequences as result of sharing their experiences on their campuses, which is, indeed, a finding in itself. We do share parts of educator participants' identities when they are relevant to the quotation. For example, we say, "Jordan, a Black woman who worked in a leadership office," but would we do not indicate the region or institutional type to protect Jordan's identity.

Student Participants

The 25 student participants' individual identities are included in Table 1.1. Figure 1.2 illustrates student participants' identities in a snapshot to provide the reader a quick overview of participants in the study.

At the time of our study, 10 student participants were graduate students, 13 were undergraduate students, and 2 were alumni who had graduated within a year of the study. Students represented 13 institutions, 12 in the United States and 1 in

TABLE 1.1 Participant Demographics

Name	*Year*	*Race*	*Gender*	*Sexuality*	*Ability*	*SES*	*Nationality*	*Additional Identities*
Alyssa	Grad	Asian American	Woman	Heterosexual	Able-bodied	Middle	American	Cambodian American
Amber	Grad	Black/African American	Woman	Straight	Able-bodied	Student	Black American	
Athena	Grad	Filipino	Woman	Straight	Lightly limited in mobility	Middle	Filipino	Immigrant
Averi	Grad	White	Agender	Queer and asexual	Non-able-bodied	Student	American	Secular and Jewish
Barbara	Grad	African American	Woman	Heterosexual	Able-bodied	Middle	American	
Beth	Undergrad	White	Woman	Heteronormative	Disabled	Lower-Middle	Canadian	
BLB	Grad	Bicultural: White Hispanic	Cisgender woman	Heterosexual	Able-bodied	Student	U.S. citizen	Hidden ethnic minority
Cora	Grad	White	Woman	Queer	Disabled	Lower-Middle	American	
Danielle	Undergrad	Black	Cisgender woman	Straight	Able	Middle	American	Christian
Eric	Undergrad	White	Man	Straight	Able-bodied	Middle	American	
Ghassan	Undergrad	Arab	Man	Heterosexual	Not disabled	Low Middle	Palestinian American	Muslim
Jamie	Undergrad	White	Woman	Bisexual	Able	Upper-middle	American	Jewish
Janet	Undergrad	White	Woman	Lesbian	Invisible Physical Disability	Middle	American	First woman in family to attend college

(*Continued*)

TABLE 1.1 (Continued)

Name	*Year*	*Race*	*Gender*	*Sexuality*	*Ability*	*SES*	*Nationality*	*Additional Identities*
Jason	Grad	Black	Man	Straight	Able	Lower	American	
Lauren	Alumni	Biracial Asian	Woman	Queer or Bi	Temporarily able-bodied	Middle	American	
Lee	Grad	White	Transgender	Pansexual	Disabled	Grad school	U.S. citizen	
Lucia	Grad	White	Genderqueer	I'm not sure. I would go with probably straight.	Non-disabled	Middle	American	Polyamorous, Veteran
Madeline	Undergrad	Black	Woman	Straight	Able-bodied	Lower-Middle	American	Christian
Marie	Undergrad	White	Woman	Lesbian	Able-bodied	Student	American	
McKenzie	Undergrad	African American & Native American	Woman	Straight	None	Prefer not to answer	African American	
Pete	Grad	South Asian	Genderqueer	Bisexual	Temporarily able-bodied	Upper	Canadian	
Rachel	Alumni	White	Woman	Straight	Able-bodied	Low-income	U.S. citizen	
Scarlet	Undergrad	White	Woman	Bisexual	Diagnosed Depression	Middle	U.S. citizen	
Teresa	Undergrad	Latina	Woman	Heterosexual	Able-bodied	Low-income	American	
Zi	Undergrad	Asian	Genderqueer	Queer	Unknown	Middle	Immigrant	

STUDENT PARTICIPANT DEMOGRAPHICS

Race

4
Asian Americans

5
Black / African Americans

3
Multiracial

11
White

1
Arab

1
Latina

Sexual Identity

14
Straight/Heterosexual

4
Queer

4
Bisexual/Pansexual

2
Lesbian

1
Unknown

Gender

17
Women

3
Men

5
Trans/Genderqueer

Institutional Type

8
Large Public Institutions

3
Small to Mid-Sized Regional Institutions

1
Historically Black University

1
Mid-Sized Private Institution

Institutional Location

5
in Georgia

4
in the Midwest

1
in Canada

2
in Mid-Atlantic

1
in the South (outside of Georgia)

EDUCATOR DEMOGRAPHICS

Race

8 White

5 Black

2 Multiracial

1 Hmong American

1 Asian American

1 Latinx

Sexual Identity

3 Gay

3 Queer

2 Bisexual/Pansexual

7 Straight

1 Questioning

1 Prefer Not to Answer

Gender

10 Women

5 Men

2 Trans/Genderqueer

Institutional Type

11 Large Public Institutions

3 Small to Mid-Sized Regional Institutions

2 Small Private Institutions

1 Large Private Institutions

Canada. Of these institutions, eight were large public institutions, three were small to mid-size regional institutions, one was an HBCU, and one a mid-size private institution. Seven institutions were located in the South, four in the Midwest, and two in the Mid-Atlantic region of the United States. Participants engaged in a variety of different activist movements, including racial justice, anti-sexual violence, queer and trans, and disability justice activism.

Fifteen participants identified as People of Color; 17 participants identified as women, 3 as men, and 5 as genderqueer; and 14 participants identified as heterosexual. Seven participants identified as having a disability, and as with all studies, participants described a complicated relationship with class. Many participants equated class with income, saying things like "poor because I'm a student," which discounts the experiences of people who are actually poor, student or not. Nine students identified as lower or lower-middle class, three declined to answer, and 13 identified as middle or upper class.

Educator Participants

Educators included people in a variety of positions, including faculty, staff, and administrators as illustrated in Figure 1.3.

Educators worked at a variety of institutional types, though large public institutions employed the majority of educator participants. We identified administrators as people at the dean or vice president level and above (e.g., dean of students, vice president for diversity and equity); staff included people who worked in student support offices (e.g., director of the LGBT resource center, coordinator for leadership programs); and faculty included people whose full-time role at the institution was teaching classes and conducting research. Participants included seven entry-level and five mid-level staff, three senior-level administrators, and two faculty members. Six participants worked directly in identity-based or diversity-related centers (i.e., multicultural center, LGBT center). Eight of the participants had earned a terminal degree (i.e., Ph.D., Ed.D.), seven had a master's degree, and two had a bachelor's degree. Nine participants identified as People of Color and eight as white; nine identified as cisgender women, six as cisgender men, and two as genderqueer. Nine identified as queer or questioning, seven as heterosexual, and one preferred not to answer.

Chapter Summary

In this chapter, we provided an overview of the context and theoretical framework guiding the development of this study. Further, we described the power-conscious framework in detail to provide insight into the ways we accounted for power throughout the data collection and analysis process. We shared our own personal journeys to this work to illuminate our positionalities and elucidate our assumptions about this work. Finally, we described the ways that we collected data and provided a brief overview of the participants in this study. In the following chapters, we provide additional context based on the literature about student activism and some historical and current discussion of student movements.

References

Adams, M. A., Blumenfeld, W. J., Castaneda, C., Hackman, H. W., Peters, M. L., & Zúñiga X. (2013). *Teaching for diversity & social justice* (pp. 21–35). New York, NY: Routledge.

Bensimon, E. M. (2007). The underestimated significance of practitioner knowledge in the scholarship on student success. *The Review of Higher Education, 30*(4), 41–469.

Boje, D. M., & Rosile, G. A. (2001). Where's the power in empowerment? Answers from Follett and Clegg. *The Journal of Applied Behavioral Science, 37*(1), 90–117.

Campbell, R. (2016, July 2). UndocuQueers: How the LGBT and immigrant rights movement progress together. *Huffington Post.* Retrieved from www.huffingtonpost.com/ryan-campbell/undocuqueers-how-the-lgbt-and-immigrant-rights-movement-progress-together_b_7689118.html

Clandinin, D. J., & Connelly, F. M. (2000). *Narrative inquiry: Experience and story in qualitative research.* San Francisco, CA: Jossey-Bass.

Delgado, R. (1989). Storytelling for oppositionists and others: A plea for narrative. *Michigan Law Review, 87*(8), 2411–2441.

Delgado, R., & Stefancic, J. (2012). *Critical race theory: An introduction* (2nd ed.). New York, NY: New York University Press.

Donat, P. L., & D'Emilio, J. (1992). A feminist redefinition of rape and sexual assault: Historical foundations and change. *Journal of Social Issues, 48*(1), 9–22.

Ferguson, R. A. (2017). *We demand: The university and student protests.* Oakland, CA: University of California Press.

Freedman, E. B. (2013). *Redefining rape: Sexual violence in the era of suffrage and segregation.* Cambridge, MA: Harvard University Press.

Freire, P. (2000/1970). *Pedagogy of the oppressed* (30th anniversary ed.). New York, NY: Continuum.

hooks, b. (1994). *Teaching to transgress: Education as the practice of freedom.* New York, NY: Routledge.

Incite! Women of Color Against Violence. (2006). *Color of violence.* Cambridge, MA: South End Press.

Johnson, A. G. (2006). *Power, privilege and difference* (2nd ed.). Boston, MA: McGraw-Hill.

Kezar, A. (2010). Faculty and staff partnering with student activists: Unexplored terrains of interaction and development. *Journal of College Student Development, 51*(5), 451–480.

Kincheloe, J. L., & McLaren, P. (2000). Rethinking critical theory and qualitative research. In N. K. Denzin, & Y. S. Lincoln (Eds.), *Handbook of qualitative research* (2nd ed., pp. 279–313). Thousand Oaks, CA: Sage.

Lindemann, B. S. (1984). "To Ravish and carnally know": Rape in eighteenth-century Massachusetts. *Signs, 10*(1), 63–82.

Linder, C. (2018). *Sexual violence on campus: Power-conscious approaches to awareness, prevention, and response.* Bingley, UK: Emerald Publishing Limited.

Linder, C., Myers, J. S., Riggle, C., & Lacy, M. (2016). From margins to mainstream: Social media as a tool for campus sexual violence activism. *Journal of Diversity in Higher Education, 9*(3), 231–244. doi:http://dx.doi.org/10.1037/dhe0000038

Linder. C., Quaye, S. J., Lange, A. C., Roberts, R. E., Lacy, M., & Okello, W. K. (2019). "A student should have the privilege of just being a student": Student activism as labor. *The Review of Higher Education, 42*, 37–62.

Lowery, W. (2017, January 17). Black lives matter: Birth of a movement. *The Guardian*. Retrieved from www.theguardian.com/us-news/2017/jan/17/black-lives-matter-birth-of-a-movement

McDowell, L. (2012, July 2). Non-hierarchical structures: Could it work for you? *The Guardian*. Retrieved from www.theguardian.com/voluntary-sector-network/2012/jul/02/charities-non-hierarchical-structures

Media Education Foundation. (1997). *Bell Hooks: Cultural criticism & transformation* [Video transcript]. Retrieved from www.mediaed.org/transcripts/Bell-Hooks-Transcript.pdf

Museus, S. D., & Neville, K. M. (2012). Delineating the ways that key institutional agents provide racial minority students with access to social capital in college. *Journal of College Student Development, 53*(3), 436–452.

Pritchard, A., & McChesney, J. (2018). Focus on student affairs, 2018: Understanding key challenges using CUPA-HR data. (Research Report). *CUPA-HR*. Retrieved from www.cupahr.org/surveys/research-briefs/.

Rhoads, R. A. (1997). Interpreting identity politics: The educational challenge of contemporary student activism. *Journal of College Student Development, 38*(5), 508–519.

Ropers-Huilman, B., Carwile, L., & Barnett, K. (2005). Student activists' characterizations of administrators in higher education: Perceptions of power in "the system". *The Review of Higher Education, 28*(3), 295–312. doi:10.1353/rhe.2005.0012

Smith, E. I. (2016, September 2). *Minority vs. minoritized* [weblog post]. Retrieved from www.theodysseyonline.com/minority-vs-minoritize

Takaki, R. (2008). *A different mirror: A history of multicultural America* (Revised Edition). New York, NY: Back Bay Books.

Tatum, B. D. (2000). Complexity of identity. In M. Adams, W. Blumenfield, R. Castaneda, H. Hackman, M. Peters, & X. Zuniga (Eds.), *Readings for diversity and social justice* (pp. 9–14). New York, NY: Routledge.

Warner, M. (1999). *The trouble with normal: Sex, politics, and the ethics of queer life*. New York, NY: Simon & Schuster.

2

HISTORICAL AND CURRENT CONTEXTS FOR IDENTITY-BASED STUDENT ACTIVISM ON U.S. COLLEGE CAMPUSES

Student activists have engaged in activism on college campuses for as long as colleges have existed. Some of the earliest traces of student activism date back to the 13th century when students in Europe formed coalitions to combat the power of the faculty (Boren, 2001). In the United States, one of the earliest documented instances of student activism is (in)famously known as the Bad Butter Rebellion at Harvard University in 1776. Dissatisfied over a decades-long decline in food quality, students rioted (Moore, 1997; Pisner, 2011). Other notable periods of student activism include the late 1930s when students protested World War II (Braungart & Braungart, 1990; Cohen, 2013); the 1960s when student activist efforts were directly tied to the larger civil rights movement in the United States (Cohen, 2013); resistance to the Vietnam War in the late 1960s and 1970s (Hine, 1996); and multicultural advocacy, reform, and transformation on campuses from the 1970s through the 1990s (Levine & Wilson, 1979; Rhoads, 1998).

A comprehensive review of the literature about identity-based student activism is beyond the scope of this book. Scholars have written more on Black student movements alone than we can review in this chapter. For a detailed, thorough understanding of various identity-based student movements, we recommend readers engage in depth with previous scholarship dedicated to specific student movements, including such works as Ibram Kendi's (2013), *The Black Campus Movement*; Susana Muñoz's (2015), *Identity, Social Activism, and the Pursuit of Higher Education: The Journey Stories of Undocumented and Unafraid Community Activists*; Joy Ann Williamson-Lott's (2018) *Jim Crow Campus: Higher Education and the Struggle for a New Southern Social Order*; and Roderick A. Ferguson's (2019) *One-Dimensional Queer.*

In this chapter, we explore a history of campus-based activism and its relationship to current organizing on college and university campuses in the United

States. To set a context for this book, we provide a brief overview of the evolution of higher education, explore the influence of identity-based student activism on institutional structures and practices, and highlight the evolution of institutional responses to identity-based student activism. We conclude by highlighting notable identity-based college student activist movements on campus between 2010 and 2018, showing how they relate to larger and broader national movements.

Evolution of Higher Education

Writing about the history of any topic is a challenging endeavor. Most recorded history is written from the perspective of dominant group members, often white, educated, male academics. Even when historical accounts center minoritized groups, including People of Color, women, queer and trans people, and people with disabilities, they often still focus on minoritized groups' experiences through lenses of dominant ways of thinking. Although we recognize this risk when writing about the history of student activism, we do our best to critically analyze the historical literature about identity-based student activism, highlighting the questions we have about who is left out and what stories are missing from the historical literature. Additionally, as highlighted in Chapter 1, we recognize our positionalities as U.S.-based academics, writing through a colonized Western lens, as much as we try to recognize and interrupt that lens.

In what is now known as the United States, wealthy, white men affiliated with churches established institutions of higher education in the late 1600s and early 1700s (Wilder, 2013). These institutions, referred to as colonial colleges, served as a place to educate elite, white men who would become clergy, doctors, lawyers, and government officials (Thelin, 2011). Although many scholars and founders of higher education have argued that the purpose of higher education was for the "public good," meaning that higher education should do the work of educating people to engage in democracy and citizenship, the public good mission of higher education has changed over time (Dorn, 2017, p. 17). Like other forms of education, higher education perpetuates social reproduction, maintaining patriarchy and white supremacy. Higher education's goal of social mobility, a goal representing education as a private good, has overtaken its public good goals. This elevation of social mobility has resulted in a focus on helping people gain affluence in the form of higher-paying jobs, access to networks of other educated people, and related individual benefits (Dorn, 2017; Labaree, 1997). Although affluence may positively impact individual people, it also creates a further divide between people who have access to higher education and those who do not, thus foreclosing higher education as the great equalizer. Without attention to the public good, higher education perpetuates continued division and social stratification.

Over time, people with minoritized identities advocated for inclusion in higher education; however, minoritized people primarily attended colleges specifically for women and/or People of Color (Cohen & Kisker, 2010; Solomon, 1985), leaving the elite institutions to maintain the status quo by continuing to educate almost exclusively white men. Not only did elite colleges exclude minoritized people, but they also accumulated significant amounts of wealth by exploiting People of Color, specifically enslaved Black and African people, to provide unpaid labor to the campuses (Wilder, 2013). Although some Indigenous people attended elite institutions as students, white men with power admitted them to support the continuation of patriarchal white supremacy. Specifically, by admitting Indigenous people to elite white institutions, leaders sought to assimilate Indigenous people to dominant white culture, resulting in more people to support the status quo (Wilder, 2013; Wright, 1988).

White women began to attend college in larger numbers in the mid-1800s and primarily attended finishing schools or normal schools where they received training to educate white boys to become elite white men (Solomon, 1985). Known as "republican motherhood," white women's roles in patriarchal white supremacy included educating children, especially boys, so that they could continue on to elite institutions and continue to effectively perpetuate the status quo by maintaining power and dominance (Solomon, 1985, p. 12). After the Civil War, Black women also began to attend college to become teachers, though because of segregation and racism, their work specifically focused on educating Black children who were not allowed in white schools (Solomon, 1985).

In 1862, U.S. Congress passed the first Morrill Act, granting land to states to establish public universities designed to provide education to more people, specifically focused on agriculture and engineering. Technically, land-grant institutions were to be open to everyone, but they primarily served middle- and working-class white people, mostly men (Cohen & Kisker, 2010). Congress passed a second Morrill Act in 1890 to provide states with funding to establish institutions of higher education specifically for formerly enslaved Black people as a strategy to keep Black students out of predominantly and historically white institutions (Cohen & Kisker, 2010). Although today Historically Black Colleges and Universities (HBCUs) serve as a temporary reprieve from white supremacy for many Black students, they began as a result of continued racism and efforts to further segregation perpetuated by white men with power in U.S. Congress.

After World War II, the culture in the United States shifted to push more students to attend all institutions of higher education, including those that had been predominantly white. Specifically, industries in the United States shifted, requiring a more skilled labor force, and the G.I. Bill of 1944 made it possible for more middle- and working-class white men to attend college after returning from the War (Cohen & Kisker, 2010). Although Men of Color and women were technically included in the G.I. Bill, white men primarily benefited from the bill (Katznelson, 2005).

As more People of Color and middle-class white people began to access higher education in the 1960s, campus leaders struggled to develop environments that welcomed and included their experiences and perspectives. Student activists demanded that administrators and educators do more to ensure diverse perspectives and experiences were welcomed on those campuses, thus identity-based student activism surged. Throughout history, identity-based student activists have connected issues in the larger culture with issues on campus, pushing educators and administrators to recognize the public good mission of institutions of higher education. As the climate in the United States continued to shift in relationship to equity and justice, student activists in the 1960s actively participated in the civil rights movement both on and off campus. Scholars often extract "Black students from their Black campus reality and [analyze] them as if their identity as activists preempted or was more important than their identities as students" (Williamson-Lott, 2018, p. 238). Divorcing students from their on-campus realities misses the complex work these activists engaged in to transform their campuses for the better. In addition to the marches, protests, and sit-ins designed to address voting rights, segregation, and other racist practices in the larger U.S. culture, student activists also pushed colleges and universities to address oppressive structures, including curricular offerings, admissions and hiring practices, and inhospitable spaces on campuses (Rhoads, 1998).

Influence of Identity-Based Student Activism on Universities

Issues of equity and inclusion manifest on U.S. college and university campuses in similar ways to the larger U.S. culture. Institutions of higher education are not insular from the environments within which they exist, and perpetuate unique forms of harm and oppression (Cho, 2018; Dixson, 2018). Despite oppressive institutional structures and practices, student activists have been instrumental in initiating a number of curricular and co-curricular changes, including the addition of women's studies and ethnic studies programs (Arthur, 2011), curricular diversity requirements (Rhoads, 2016), and the addition of cultural centers and culturally based student organizations on campuses (Patton, 2010; Stewart, 2011).

Minoritized students generally do not have the luxury of choosing to engage in either on-campus or off-campus activism; their lives as minoritized people are impacted by systemic oppression no matter where they are. In fact, many minoritized people engage in activism by way of existence and resistance on a daily basis, resulting in their activism starting long before they come to college campuses as everyday existence (Dixson, 2018). Many people do not consider resistance and existence activism because they do not always take the popular form of marches, sit-ins, and protests, yet some people's mere existence in a space not designed for them results in change. Existence as resistance is a form of activism that scholars and others sometimes fail to acknowledge. With this nuance in mind, we move forward in this section by highlighting some of the ways identity-based student activism connects with issues in the larger culture and how some identity-based student activism appears repetitive because leaders of institutions of higher education fail to effectively address and transform systems of oppression (Cho, 2018; Dixson, 2018).

Racial Justice Activism

Perhaps some of the most oft-cited examples of students engaging in activism are from the civil rights movement of the 1960s. Not only did students engaged in marches and sit-ins off-campus to address issues of segregation, voting rights, and equitable access to resources including housing and education, but they also translated those actions to campuses where they demanded more inclusive curriculum, an increase in Black faculty and staff, and more hospitable campus environments (Reuben, 1998; Williamson, 2003). This trend remains true today; Black student activism on college and university campuses closely connects with the movement for Black Lives, or #BlackLivesMatter activism, in larger society (Dixson, 2018). Perhaps not surprisingly, Black student activists' demands are similar today as they were in the 1960s (Bradley, 2016; Patton, 2015), indicating that although college and university administrators made some progress in addressing student concerns in the 1960s, there is still much to be addressed.

Similarly, during the civil rights movement of the 1960s, Latin@/x students also demanded an improved curriculum and increased inclusivity in P–16 education (Delgado Bernal, 1998). Although the Chican@/x and Latin@/x movements do not receive the same level of attention in scholarship or popular media coverage as Black student movements, they happened around the same time and made connections between campus and societal matters, including issues of access and equity in education and issues around immigration and citizenship (Delgado Bernal, 1998). Similar to activist demands concerning anti-Blackness, student organizing related to issues of concern for Latin@/x students have also been circular. Latin@/x students today are still demanding equitable access to education, including more attention to citizenship issues, again indicating that institutions of higher education have not made much progress (DeAngelo, Schuster, & Stebleton, 2016; Hope, Keels, & Durkee, 2016).

The development of ethnic studies and women's studies programs is an example of identity-based activists working in solidarity with each other. Although most of the scholarship about ethnic studies courses focuses on the addition of Black and Latin@/x studies (Arthur, 2011; Rhoads, 1998), Asian and Indigenous students also pushed universities to add a variety of ethnically based curricula in the form of courses, departments, and majors. Despite a history of racism and white supremacy in some aspects of the women's movement and a legacy of sexism in some aspects of racial justice organizing, faculty and students from different ethnic backgrounds often worked together to build academic programs around the same time (Arthur, 2011; Rhoads, 1998). For example, although there was some division among Asian American students about racial justice and civil rights initiatives, many Asian Americans came to a deeper understanding of American imperialism as a result of the Vietnam war, which corresponded with the civil rights movement in the United States (Nguyen & Gasman, 2015). The timing of these movements resulted in some Asian students and Black students working in solidarity to raise consciousness about issues of racism and imperialism and to establish Black studies and Asian studies programs on a number of campuses.

Disability Justice Activism

In the late 1960s, students with disabilities also engaged in heightened activism around access to higher education. Although the Americans with Disabilities Act did not become law until 1990, students with physical disabilities organized to demand access to classrooms and campus activities much earlier. For instance, in the 1960s at the University of California, Berkeley, a group called the Rolling Quads worked to establish the floor of a campus hospital as housing for disabled students. The students continued their activism by organizing "to combat the paternalistic managerial practices of the university and the California Department of Rehabilitation" (Dansforth, 2018, p. 506). Specifically, the students pushed the university and the Department of Rehabilitation to consider the possibility of students with disabilities successfully participating in college. The student activists used a variety of tactics to engage their activism including working within the system to appease administrators by using their language and justification, including using college as a training ground to help people with disabilities become more independent, and engaging in direct action, including letter writing campaigns and involving media to tell their stories (Dansforth, 2018). Eventually, student activism resulted in more accessible campuses for students with disabilities and contributed to the passage of the Americans with Disabilities Act of 1990.

Activism to Address Sexism

Much of recorded history about the so-called women's movement highlights college and university campuses as the birthplace of that movement, spotlighting the 1970s as the birth of activism around sexual harassment and violence (Bohmer & Parrot, 1993). However, more critical scholarship challenged these notions by illustrating the ways Black women have been organizing around issues of sexism and sexual violence for centuries, and that college campuses are where white, middle-class women's activism around sexual violence began (McGuire, 2010). This being said, the relationship between women's movements on college and university campuses and the larger context in the United States cannot be denied. Activists on college and university campuses were instrumental in advancing issues of equity and justice related to gender. Similar to the racial justice activists in the 1960s, feminist activists in the 1970s raised awareness about chilly campus climates for women students, faculty, and staff (Hall & Sandler, 1982), and successfully advocated for the passage of Title IX in 1972. Further, activists on college campuses also facilitated their fair share of consciousness-raising groups, designed to provide a space for women to discuss and process their previously unnamed experiences with sexism. Women's centers were established on a number of college and university campuses in the 1970s and 1980s in response to the research emerging and highlighting lack of physical safety for women students, and the ways women faculty, staff, and students experienced sexism on campus.

LGBT Justice Activism

Many people credit the Stonewall Riots in 1969 as the beginning of the public activism around sexuality and, to a lesser extent, gender issues; similarly, some students on college and university campuses organized around the harm and exclusion of lesbian, gay, and bisexual (LGB) students during this same time period (Bailey, 1999; Beemyn, 2003; Clawson, 2014). Although most higher education scholarship points to the 1990s as the height of LGB activism on campuses (Rhoads, 1998; Rhoads, 2016), students in the 1970s fought back against homophobic university policies and practices expelling gay students (or students who were perceived to be gay) from campus (Bailey, 1999; Beemyn, 2003; Clawson, 2014; Reichard, 2010). Similarly, despite university policies banning them and the danger of being physically harmed by homophobic students and police, gay students also organized social events to celebrate and raise awareness about issues of significance to them (Ferguson, 2019).

In the 1960s and 1970s, a number of campuses engaged in "the purging of gay students" (Nash & Silverman, 2015, p. 443), meaning that they began to follow their codes of conduct and expel (or threaten to expel) students who were gay or perceived to be gay. Gay and lesbian students, however, refused to be silenced or ignored. An example of existence as resistance, queer students fought for recognition on their campuses. For example, in 1972, students at the University of Georgia organized the Big Gay Dance as a form of awareness raising on campus. Two students founded the Committee on Gay Education, then within four months of its founding, jumped through hoops to reserve a ballroom in the campus union and advertise the dance. Despite threats of violence from the Ku Klux Klan and threats of expulsion from university administrators, the activists held the dance in the student union anyway (Bartunek, 2016).

The 1990s brought another surge of organizing around LGB issues, resulting in some campuses establishing LGB resource centers, many of which evolved to LGBT resource centers over time. Despite the name change, many of these centers do not effectively serve transgender students as they are frequently included as an afterthought; often, these offices programs are *about*, rather than *for*, transgender students (Marine & Nicolazzo, 2014).

As student activists organized around issues of equity and inclusion on campus, administrators and educators took on a variety of roles to engage them. Depending on their roles and social identities, administrators and educators have navigated a number of tensions and experiences in their efforts to engage with student activists, sometimes as advocates and sometimes as barriers to the activists' efforts.

Evolution of Institutional Support of Student Activism

Scholarship on the role of educators and administrators engaging with student activists is sparse and rarely focuses exclusively on identity-based activism and/or power. Early work on the role of educators supporting student activists illustrates the changing roles of student affairs professionals in relation to *in loco parentis* (Wolf-Wendel, Twombly, Tuttle, Ward, & Gaston-Gayles, 2004). More recent scholarship on the role of educators' relationships with student activists examines the struggles that administrators and educators manage (Harrison, 2010, 2014) and ways that faculty may partner with student activists to create change on campus (Kezar, 2010). In this section, we trace the evolution of student affairs educators' roles in supporting student activists from the civil rights movement to today.

Civil Rights Movement

Although early scholarship on the role of educators and administrators supporting student activists rarely accounts for or addresses issues of identity, a close reading of historical accounts of student activism highlights the ways identity and consciousness influenced educators and administrators' relationships with students. For example, when the University of Georgia first desegregated, student activists engaged in a number of strategies to create safer and more equitable environments on campus. Pratt (2002) interviewed administrators, students, and policymakers present during the period of desegregation and illustrated the various ways different administrators supported student activists. The majority of university administrators and policymakers were wealthy white men (Pratt, 2002). Some of these men listened to student activists, striving to support them in their efforts to create a safer campus, while the majority of administrators resisted students' demands and sided with the status quo in the state, perpetuating white supremacy and racism by failing to acknowledge or perpetuating an unsafe campus environment for Black students (Pratt, 2002). Conversely, Black administrators across the country acknowledged the ways their racial identity influenced their work with students, including making them more aware of the issues students were organizing around (Wolf-Wendel et al., 2004) and more of a target for white administrators and policymakers (Cole, 2018).

During the civil rights movement of the 1960s, the role of student affairs professionals quickly ascended in importance at colleges and universities (Wolf-Wendel et al., 2004). Alongside the civil rights movement, students also advocated for and successfully changed university policies related to student discipline and privacy. Up to this point, college and university administrators acted *in loco parentis* (in place of the parent) and managed students' affairs in paternalistic, hands-on ways. In the 1960s, students also demanded more privacy and independence. The combination of students engaging in civil rights activism and the push for more privacy on campus resulted in the emergence of due process practices in conduct. Scholars describe *Dixson v. Alabama* as a "landmark case" defining due process rights of students (Swem, 1987, p. 359). Administrators at Alabama State College expelled five students for participating in the civil rights movement without notice or a hearing. The U.S. Supreme Court ruled that expelling students with no notice or hearing was unconstitutional at institutions receiving federal funding, thus instituting due process on college and university campuses (Swem, 1987). Changes in students' rights resulted in student affairs educators' roles changing from being intimately involved in students' personal lives to serving the institution in more of an administrative and management role. For example, administrators had to distance themselves from the personal issues that students may bring to them related to discipline so as to remain objective during disciplinary hearings.

During this period, the expertise of student affairs educators in managing crises and understanding student development benefited university presidents who had little experience in working with students (Wolf-Wendel et al., 2004). With the increase in profile for student affairs educators came a shift in their responsibility to the institution, creating some challenges navigating their loyalty to students they served and their loyalty to the institutions and presidents that employed them (Wolf-Wendel et al., 2004). Student affairs educators during the civil rights era identified themselves as "disciplinarian; advocate, mentor, and friend; educator and resource; mediator; initiator, and change agent" (Gaston-Gayles, Wolf-Wendel, Tuttle, Twombly, & Ward, 2005, p. 268), sometimes wearing multiple hats at the same time.

Given their now complex and sometimes contradictory roles, student affairs educators navigated a variety of challenging environments at their institutions during the civil rights movement. For example, one of the primary roles that student affairs educators felt pressured to accept was that of disciplinarian and, for the most part, they believed in the significance and educational power of that role. However, on some occasions, they worried that presidents expected them to enact their role as a disciplinarian to make the university look good and not "offend trustees" (Gaston-Gayles et al., 2005, p. 269) more than to educate students. Further, their roles as advocates for students sometimes conflicted with their colleagues' perspectives about maintaining the status quo. As described by James Rhatigan, dean of students and vice president for student affairs at Wichita State University in Kansas, "I went to work when others said no to a student. When people said no to a student, this was often infuriating to me. Usually I took the view that the student's issue was legitimate, unless proven otherwise." He continued saying that they may not be helping students because "we were just too damn lazy or set in our ways" (Wolf-Wendel et al., 2004, p. 338). Finally, student affairs professionals took their role as educators with student activists seriously.

They shared stories of helping students navigate institutional bureaucracies and sharing "tools of protest" with them (Wolf-Wendel et al., 2004, p. 240).

Although scholarship about the roles of student affairs educators in the civil rights movement does not specifically address the role of educators through an identity- or power-conscious lens, the majority of participants in Wolf-Wendel et al.'s (2004) study on the role of student affairs educators identified as white, and one can assume that many of the student activists they supported during this time period identified as Students of Color, likely most often Black students. The Black educators and administrators in the study did describe the ways their racial identity influenced their work with students, but none of the white educators appeared to discuss their race (or at least the authors did not discuss whiteness in their write up of the study; Wolf-Wendel et al., 2004; Gaston-Gayles et al., 2005).

Current Contexts

More recent scholarship about the role of educators supporting student activists examines the relationship between students and faculty to address campus climate issues and examines the ways staff navigate politics and institutional power in their roles. Specifically, Kezar (2010) interviewed 165 faculty, staff, and administrators at a variety of institutional types to better understand the relationships among students, faculty, and staff as they relate to grassroots activism. Kezar (2010) highlighted the significance of institutional context on the relationships among faculty, staff, and students and illustrated various ways educators worked with students to engage in grassroots activism. Similar to the Wolf-Wendel and colleagues' study (2004), participants highlighted their roles as mediators, behind the scenes activists, educators, and front-line activists in their work with students. However, Kezar (2010) did not discuss participants' social identities, leaving us to wonder how power and participants' social identities influenced the findings.

Many student affairs staff members describe the challenges of navigating power in institutional contexts as part of their roles in supporting students. For example, while student affairs educators have been socialized and trained to support students, sometimes this role of student support conflicts with the expectation from university administrators (including presidents) to maintain control and calm in a campus environment (Harrison & Mather, 2017; McElderry & Hernandez Rivera, 2017). As student affairs educators strive to develop ways to navigate this tension, the consequences are different for educators with minoritized identities, especially when they share those identities with the students (McElderry & Hernandez Rivera, 2017). For example, Black educators share significant experiences with isolation, exhaustion, and invisibility while supporting student activists (McElderry & Hernandez Rivera, 2017), whereas white activists do not report similar experiences (Harrison & Mather, 2017).

Very little scholarship explicitly examines the experiences of minoritized faculty and staff as they relate to supporting student activists. The limited scholarship highlights the ways minoritized faculty and staff engage in emotional labor in supporting student activists who share their identities and feel isolated and unsupported by their institutions in doing this work (McElderry & Hernandez Rivera, 2017; Quaye, Shaw, & Hill, 2017). For example, two Black administrators at the University of Missouri shared their experiences attempting to support Black students during the publicly visible activism related to racism at Mizzou in the fall of 2015. They shared experiencing isolation, exhaustion, silencing, taxation, and invisibility as a result of their work with students. Specifically, they noted that colleagues rarely checked in with them during heightened times of protest and danger on campus, resulting in them feeling both isolated and unsafe. Additionally, when they supported students in working with administrators, one author shared how his experience "created taxation" for him in that he "needed to do more work pre- and post-interaction [with administrators], in that I had to prepare students, but also take care of them once their interaction was over" (McElderry & Hernandez Rivera, 2017, p. 329).

Unfortunately, the activism most supported by institutional leaders via resources and active verbal support is student activism that focuses on issues off-campus, rather than issues affecting students on campus (Linder, 2019). For example, college and university administrators tend to respond well to student activism that has a clear, direct connection to traditional notions of democracy and civic engagement, including service-learning, volunteering, and "helping" people off-campus (Boyte, 2008, p. 13). Perhaps not coincidentally, white women students dominate the research about most service-learning and volunteer programs (see Biddix, 2010; Dominguez, 2009; Linder, Myers, Riggle, & Lacy, 2016; Taha, Hastings, & Minei, 2015; Winston, 2013). Many of these service-learning and volunteer programs, designed through an individualistic lens, train students to focus more on helping others than on transforming systems and structures that cause oppression and harm. Although many service-learning programs have attempted to shift the focus from individuals to systems (Boyte, 2008), this shift in culture proves challenging because of the ways wealthy, white, Christian students engaged in these programs are socialized and rewarded at an individual level for helping, rather than transforming systems from which they benefit. Volunteer work fits nicely on a resume and in a graduate school admissions essay, while engaging in transformative resistance may actually hurt students' chances of getting into college or graduate school (e.g., Thornhill, 2018). Additionally, transforming cultures and systems requires that people with privilege understand and let go of some of those privileges, which is lifelong work, not something that can be done in a one-time volunteer engagement or even a semester-long civic learning course.

Students engaged in identity-based or power-conscious activism, or activism aimed at interrupting and transforming systems of oppression, typically receive less support from their institutions. Often, students engage in identity-based and power-conscious activism around issues that directly impact their experiences on campus and are therefore in direct tension with campus administrators and some educators. However, despite this tension, identity-based student activists have historically and consistently influenced campus structures and environments, including curricular and co-curricular practices. Next, we examine identity-based student activist movements between 2010 and 2018 to provide a current context for the chapters in the remainder of this book.

Current Context for Identity-Based Student Activism

In this section, we highlight a few notable campus protests and movements as a way to illustrate a pathway to identity-based student activism on college and university campuses. The events highlighted are not meant to be an exhaustive list of all relevant college and university movements. First, we will set the stage for student activism in the current context, then highlight specific areas in which student activists have been organizing.

Setting the Stage: Hatred and Bigotry in National Politics

Several incidents in the 2010s laid the groundwork for what would ultimately be a swell of identity-based student activism over the next several years. In 2009, the conservative Tea Party wing of the Republican Party gained formal power with the election of officials to the U.S. Congress and threatened to shut down the government in 2011, succeeding in 2013 because of their desire to defund the Affordable Care Act (Amadeo, 2018). Not only did their chosen name, a nod to the Boston Tea Party, invoke historical violence against Indigenous communities, their ideologies and policy platforms directly impacted minoritized communities in negative ways, including perpetuating overtly racist ideologies at rallies and protests across the country (Maxwell, 2016). Further, anti-immigrant sentiments in the United States grew during this time, leading to increased deportations of undocumented people (Slevin, 2010). Around this same time period, students engaged in activism related to multiple social issues, including launching LGBT advocacy and anti-bullying campaigns, raising attention related to student loan debt through the Occupy Wall Street movement, advocating for access to education for undocumented students raised in the United States (Muñoz, 2015), and taking part in the beginnings of police accountability movements (Goyette & Rothberg, 2011; Greenlaw, 2017).

The highly contested 2016 U.S. national election, its unprecedented tone, and the ultimate outcome sent waves across every corner of the United States and around the world. During the campaign, then-candidate Donald Trump deliberately engaged in forms of dog-whistle politics that helped tap into and embolden white nationalists and supremacists around the world (Holston, 2016). In addition to a rise in hate crimes both on and off college campuses around the country (Bauman, 2016), Trump made campaign promises for "border security" laced with insults and negative rhetoric about Mexican people, calling them drug dealers and rapists (Ye He Lee, 2015). Further, an audio recording of Trump engaging in vulgar conversation about his treatment of women emerged. Despite this hateful and harmful discourse directed at People of Color and immigrants and behavior directed at women, he was elected. When white supremacists swarmed the campus of the University of Virginia, Trump defended them and the spirit of their actions by describing them as "very fine people" (Scott, 2018).

This hateful rhetoric and behavior prompted an increase in student activism across the United States. Students at Colorado College, the University of Michigan, UC San Diego, UCLA, and the University of Texas, Austin, organized events in an effort to combat the hateful and divisive rhetoric from the election season (Jaschik, 2016; Pauker, 2016). Further, Cornell University students, along with several activist groups across the country, organized "The People's Walkout," where students of all ages walked out of their classrooms in protest of hate speech spewed during the entirety of the election (Subramaniam, 2016). Against this backdrop, we provide an overview of contemporary student movements and their relationship to the larger national context.

The Movement for Black Lives

One of the first major events fueling identity-based movements was the murder of Trayvon Martin in Sanford, Florida, in 2012. Viewed by many as a hate-crime riddled with racism and bias, demonstrations swept across the United States in reaction to Martin's murder, including on college campuses. For example, students at Virginia Tech hosted a Hoodie March to raise awareness about Trayvon's case (Heineck, 2012), a nod to the fact that Trayvon was gunned down in a hoodie. The hoodie became symbolic for the ways police and other authorities often treat Black people as a problem through profiling and unfair judgment before being treated as people. At The Ohio State University, unknown people vandalized the Black Cultural Center with the message "Long Live Zimmerman" in support of George Zimmerman, the gunman who murdered Trayvon. Students at OSU demonstrated to raise awareness about Martin's case and to address campus climate issues around race and racism. Their demonstrations led to the establishment and implementation of a campus hate crime alert as well as several anti-hate/anti-bias initiatives at the university (Stewart & Quaye, 2019).

On July 13, 2013, the jury in the Zimmerman trial rendered a not-guilty verdict and Alicia Garza, Patrisse Cullors, and Opal Tometi founded the #BlackLivesMatter movement (Black Lives Matter, n.d.). The growing visibility of violence against Black people, from Oscar Grant in 2010, to Trayvon Martin in 2012, and Kimani Gray in 2013 (Abel, 2014), resulted in riots in East Flatbush, New York (Mathias, 2013). By 2014, the national movement for Black Lives was in high gear, not only in major cities across the United States, but also on college campuses. On August 9, 2014, after a white police officer shot and killed Mike Brown of Ferguson, Missouri (Brown, 2014), a clear uptick in organizing and activism around police violence emerged. The Mike Brown case was an example not only of police and state violence against often innocent and unarmed Black victims, but also of the subsequent militarization of police in Ferguson. The work of local activists put Mike Brown's case and issues around police violence on a national stage. College students planned protests and demonstrations on campuses across the country, most notably at St. Louis University and the University of Missouri, the latter of which would lead to #ConcernedStudent1950 in 2015 (Izadi, 2015).

Black students at the University of Missouri repeatedly vocalized negative experiences they endured while being on campus, including being called the N-word and the lack of any response by university administrators to what was happening in Ferguson (Izadi, 2015). They established #ConcernedStudent1950, referring to the year Black students were admitted to the institution, and received more backlash from insensitive and intolerant community members. Jonathan Butler, a graduate student, helped organize many activist efforts on the campus and increased the intensity of the protests when he went on a seven-day hunger strike (Crawford, 2015). Additional demonstrations eventually led to a strike by the football team and resignation of Tim Wolfe, the University of Missouri system president (Izadi, 2015).

The events at Mizzou resonated nationwide as activists and organizers worked to plan events that aimed to show solidarity to students and their cause at Mizzou while also highlighting the ways other college and universities suffer from racist environments. Students at Yale University, Ithaca College, the University of Wisconsin–Milwaukee, and Colorado State University all held rallies, protests, and demonstrations on their campuses (Chung & Payne, 2015). Student organizer Vance Payne at Colorado State offered,

> The end goal was to hope that Mizzou knows that people are moving, and people are with them. The second part is not only to support them, but to honor their movement by not being voiceless. By voicing what's going on at Mizzou, by voicing what's going on in the country, by voicing what's going on this campus; what has happened and what is *still* happening.
>
> *(CTV 11, 2015; emphasis added)*

The organizing at Mizzou birthed movements, protests, and rallies across the country on college and university campuses. The resistant actions and organizing in Ferguson after the murder of Mike Brown primed the work at Mizzou. This is one illustration of how issues in the national discourse directly impacted students on college campuses and gave them the gumption and inspiration to engage in identity-based student activism.

By mid-2016, college students made visible a strong and consistent tide of national conversations pertaining to equity and justice in the United States. The movement for Black Lives remained highly relevant and necessary as unarmed

Black people continued to suffer at the hands of police and state violence. The high-profile murders of Philando Castile, Alton Sterling, Freddie Gray, and Terrence Crutcher and subsequent lack of action by local, regional, and national legislators and politicians resulted in significant outrage at the prevalence of police violence (Park & Lee, 2017). The questionable circumstances around the death of Sandra Bland in 2015 gave momentum to the #SayHerName movement (founded in 2014; AAFP, n.d.). Noting the heavy focus on Black men in the movement for Black Lives, the founders of #SayHerName sought to raise public consciousness concerning how Black women and girls also experience police and state violence. As a result of #SayHerName, the stories of Korryn Gaines, Rekia Boyd, and the 13 Black women raped by Daniel Holtzclaw gained national attention for the ways Black and Brown girls experience violence (Whaley, 2016). The Sandra Bland case hit college students particularly hard as Bland was returning to her alma mater to work on campus when she was pulled over by a police officer (Griffin, 2015). In addition to raising attention about the ways Black women experience violence at the hands of police, the #SayHerName movement has also embraced raising awareness about the ways Black trans women experience exceptionally high rates of violence in society at large as a result of the collective failure of policymakers to acknowledge the dangerous intersections of transphobia, misogyny, and anti-Blackness (Brown, Ray, Summers, & Fraistat, 2017).

Campus-Based Sexual Violence

In addition to racism being named as an issue on campus, student activists also spotlighted sexual violence on a national stage on college campuses. In 2013, Andrea Pino, a student, and Annie Clark, an alumnae, of the University of North Carolina (UNC), organized to file a complaint with the Office of Civil Rights (OCR) about the way UNC–Chapel Hill handled allegations of sexual violence (Mangan, 2018). Pino and Clark's complaint was the first to be filed by students with no lawyers involved; soon after, other students began filing complaints with the Office of Civil Rights. Along with fellow activist Sophie Karasek, Pino and Clark started the organization End Rape on Campus (EROC) to assist college students in filing OCR complaints and other efforts to hold their campuses accountable for addressing sexual violence on campus (End Rape on Campus, n.d.). As of April 1, 2019, 502 complaints had been filed with the OCR, through both the leadership of EROC and other mechanisms (Chronicle of Higher Education, n.d.). Around the same time, student activists established the organization Know Your IX to "empower students to end sexual and dating violence in their schools" through education and policy enforcement (Know Your IX, n.d., para 1).

Also in 2013, Emma Sulkowicz gained national attention after she decided to carry her residence hall mattress with her each day on campus until her rapist was expelled, an action that was both a form of protest and also part of her senior performance art thesis (Bogler, 2016). Nearly seven months after a classmate sexually assaulted her, Sulkowicz's case was finally heard by the university, and ultimately her attacker was not held responsible (Frej, 2014).

A month later, college students around the world hosted various "Carry the Weight" events where they intended to show solidarity with Sulkowicz and to speak about their own experiences with sexual violence on campus. Students demonstrated at Connecticut College, UC Berkeley, Agnes Scott College, Appalachian State University, the University of Michigan, Northwestern University, Penn State, Syracuse University, Rutgers, and Harvard (Svokos, 2014). Students from more than 130 campuses committed to bringing out their mattresses and illuminated that three years after the federal government took action to increase accountability for college and university leaders to more effectively address sexual violence, they still had a long way to go toward properly addressing campus-based sexual violence.

In the fall of 2014, President Barack Obama established the White House Task Force to Protect Students from Sexual Assault as a response to student activism around sexual violence. The task force ignited a fire for college and university administrators to do a better job responding to sexual violence on college and university campuses. In February 2015, filmmakers released *The Hunting Ground*, which showcased examples of institutional betrayal, or the failure of institutional leaders to appropriately respond to allegations of sexual violence on their campuses (Dargis, 2015).

Activists have continued organizing around issues of sexual violence and harassment through ongoing campaigns similar to #MeToo and #TimesUp on the (inter)national stage. Students and faculty have organized to raise awareness about sexual harassment and violence in the academy, perpetuated by powerful faculty members and administrators. Using social media and other forms of technology, some women have begun to collect information on people who have been publicly accused of sexual harassment and the outcomes of their cases (Flaherty, 2018; Flaherty, 2017). Student and faculty activists will likely need to continue to raise attention to sexual assault and harassment for many years to come.

Activism to Address Xenophobia

The United States has a contentious history with immigration. Although the colonization of what is now predominantly referred to as the United States included people moving to this country from Europe, many people fail to consider that when addressing issues of immigration in the United States. Prior to 1995, six states (California, Florida, Illinois, New Jersey, New York, and Texas) contained three-fourths of the immigrant population in the United States (Anrig & Wang, 2006). Since then, immigration has continued to occupy a place in national discourse related to criminality, deservingness, and merit, including in conversations about access to higher education (Reich & Barth, 2010). Since 2001, immigration discourse has reeked of racist and xenophobic rhetoric primarily aimed at those from Latin and South America, fueled in part by the rhetoric of federal politicians (Kramer, 2018). The September 11, 2001, attack on U.S. soil sparked a new round of xenophobic policies related to immigration, which still have an impact on campus policies and practices today (Raghunathan, 2017). Days before the attacks, then-President Bush and Mexican president Vicente Fox jointly endorsed an immigration framework both countries could abide by the year's end; however, the September 11 attacks placed emphasis on the means by which people gained access to the country through borders (Rosenblum, 2011).

More recently, after the 2016 U.S. presidential election, Trump followed through on his promise to institute a travel ban that essentially operated as a way to target Muslims of many different nationalities and limit their ability to travel freely or safely from particular countries to the United States (Jarrett & Tatum, 2017). Students from across the country joined protesters at airports, working to raise awareness about the travel ban and to advocate for the release of people detained under the new ban (Gambino, Siddiqui, Owen, & Helmore, 2017; Kilgallen, 2017).

Student activists, documented and undocumented, have actively organized around issues of citizenship for decades—specifically advocating for policies that would allow undocumented students to continue their education in the United States and earn a path to citizenship through education (Muñoz, 2015). In 2012, after Congress failed to pass the Development, Relief, and Education for Alien Minors (DREAM) Act, which would have provided a path to citizenship for certain immigrants brought to the United States as children, President Obama signed an executive order implementing the Deferred Action for Childhood Arrivals (DACA) program. DACA defers deportation for children who were brought to the United States illegally as children. In the absence of state-level efforts to grant access, undocumented students around the country relied on DACA to attend institutions of higher education (Robertson, 2018). In recent years, however, student activists have had to re-assert their concerns as the Trump Administration announced that it would end DACA in 2017. Combined with the travel ban of 2016, the climate for international and undocumented students in the United States deteriorated quickly, resulting in increased activism on campuses related to issues of immigration. For instance, students at Syracuse University and multiple institutions in Illinois—including Northwestern University and the University of Illinois—organized protests, demonstrations, and advocacy to urge campus leaders to designate their spaces as sanctuary campuses (McMahon, 2016; Rhoads, 2016).

Student activists have met mixed results from campus administrators—while some campus administrators swiftly announced that they would not comply with the federal government's requests for names of undocumented or international students from so-called Muslim countries (Fain, 2017), others did not act at all. In fact, some campuses require faculty and staff to sign "loyalty oaths," indicating that they will uphold state and federal laws, including those banning undocumented students from state institutions (Stirgus, 2018).

Indigenous Activism

In addition to the many issues that the election brought to the fore in the national college student activist conversation, some students organized around the No Dakota Access Pipeline (NoDAPL) effort. In 2016, members of the Sioux Tribe established camps to protect the land and water that the U.S. government and Dallas-based Energy Transfer Partners threatened (Hersher, 2017). Government and energy partners wanted to construct a pipeline that would carry half a million barrels of oil through the Sioux reservation, under Lake Oahe through Iowa, and ultimately to a distribution point in Illinois. Pipeline builders proposed constructing the pipeline in an area that serves as the drinking water for many members of the Sioux Tribe (Hersher, 2017).

The protectors and allies ultimately faced off against law enforcement and the North Dakota National Guard. A violent and brutal encounter, the faceoff brought center stage how Indigenous peoples in the United States continue to experience trauma as a result of state violence. Students at several colleges and universities organized protests and demonstrations to support the Sioux Tribe, protectors of the land and the water. Students at the University of Rochester hosted a "Human Oil Spill" event in support of Standing Rock (Goodman, 2016), while students at the University of Dayton hosted a sleep out for the pipeline protest (Filby, 2016), demanding that the violence against the Sioux Tribe and against Indigenous people broadly must stop.

While support for the protectors of Standing Rock was significant, many Native American/Indigenous students noted how the violence and subjugation of the protectors was similar to what happens on college campuses. For example, in 2018, a white woman called the police on two Indigenous teens who joined a campus admission tour late because they made her uncomfortable (Associated Press, 2018). She described the teens as "odd" and indicated their quiet disposition and dark clothing were unnerving to her. Campus police stopped and questioned the teens. The profiling, surveillance, and overall negative experience they had that day illuminated that many members of college and university campuses fail to support or understand minoritized students (Associated Press, 2018). Student activists and their supporters raised awareness about this injustice by sharing it through social media, requiring the institution to respond and to more effectively train their staff and police officers on addressing issues of racism (Chappell, 2018).

Conclusion

An abundance of identity-based student activist protests, sit-ins, and demonstrations on college campuses over the past 10 years demonstrates the significance of oppression and harm in the lives of college students. Further, an increase in the numbers of Students of Color, queer and trans students, and students with disabilities on college and university campuses exemplifies the significance of existence as resistance as a significant form of activism. In many instances, the momentum behind student activism was directly tied to national and international movements where people worked to disrupt and advocate for themselves in relation to racism, sexism, xenophobia, and police and state violence in the United States. These students illuminate that colleges and universities are not exempt from reproducing oppression, dominance, and violence that exist in society more broadly. Activists have also demonstrated a commitment to ensuring institutional leaders understand their roles in addressing oppression.

Power, dominance, and oppression are woven into the fabric of the United States as well as in institutions of higher education. College student activists find themselves in especially contentious times given the various changes in the national and international landscape, including overt hatred and bigotry that surfaced during the 2016 U.S. election. The rise of Trump, the continued growth of #BlackLivesMatter, a more deliberate focus on decolonial ethics in justice work, and a more vivid illumination of power-conscious analyses on sexual violence have been front and center in activism, mobilizing, and organizing efforts. We situate our study within this context to explore the experiences of college students and their identity-based student activism as well as the educators on campus who try to support them. In the next chapter, we provide an overview of several key conceptual frameworks to pair with these contexts to inform the understanding of the findings shared in Part II of the book.

References

AAFP. (n.d.). *About the campaign*. Retrieved from http://aapf.org/about-the-campaign

Abel, K. (2014, April 3). *8 unarmed black males other than Trayvon Martin who were recently killed*. Retrieved from https://atlantablackstar.com/2014/04/03/8-unarmed-black-males-other-than-trayvon-martin-who-were-recently-killed/

Amadeo, K. (2018, December 19). The tea party movement, its economic platform, and history. *The Balance*. Retrieved from www.thebalance.com/tea-party-movement-economic-platform-3305571

Anrig, G., & Wang, T. A. (Eds.). (2006). *Immigration's new frontiers: Experiences from the emerging gateway states*. Washington, DC: Century Foundation.

Arthur, M. L. (2011). *Student activism and curricular change in higher education*. Surrey, UK: Ashgate Publishing Group.

Associated Press. (2018, May 13). Teens' experience at Colorado State shows campus reality for Native Americans. *NBC News*. Retrieved from www.nbcnews.com/news/us-news/teens-experience-colorado-state-shows-campus-reality-native-americans-n873756

Bailey, B. (1999). *Sex in the heartland*. Cambridge, MA: Harvard University Press.

Bartunek, C. J. (2016, February 6). This gay dance in Georgia in 1972 changed the world. *The Big Roundtable*. Retrieved from https://theweek.com/articles/603177/gay-dance-georgia-1972-changed-world

Bauman, D. (2018, February 16). After 2016 election, campus hate crimes seemed to jump. Here's what the data tell us. *The Chronicle of Higher Education*. Retrieved from www.chronicle.com/article/After-2016-Election-Campus/242577

Beemyn, B. (2003). The silence is broken: A history of the first lesbian, gay, and bisexual college student groups. *Journal of the History of Sexuality, 12*(2), 205–223.

Biddix, J. P. (2010). Technology uses in campus activism from 2000 to 2008: Implications for civic learning. *Journal of College Student Development, 51*(6), 679–693. doi: https://doi.org/10.1353/csd.2010.0019

Black Lives Matter. (n.d.). *Herstory*. Retrieved from https://blacklivesmatter.com/about/herstory/

Bogler, E. (2016, September 1). Emma Sulkowicz's performance art draws support from campus activists. *Columbia Spectator*. Retrieved from www.columbiaspectator.com/news/2014/09/02/emma-sulkowiczs-performance-art-draws-support-campus-activists/

Bohmer, C., & Parrot, A. (1993). *Sexual assault on campus: The problem and the solution*. New York, NY: Maxwell Macmillan International.

Boren, M. E. (2001). *Student resistance: A history of the unruly subject*. New York, NY: Routledge.

Boyte, H. C. (2008). Against the current: Developing the civic agency of students. *Change: The Magazine of Higher Education, 40*(3), 8–15.

Bradley, S. M. (2016, February 1). Black activism on campus. *The New York Times*. Retrieved from www.nytimes.com/interactive/2016/02/07/education/edlife/Black-HIstory-Activism-on-Campus-Timeline.html#/#time393_11363

Braungart, R. C., & Braungart, M. M. (1990). Political generational themes in the American student movements of the 1930s and 1960s. *Journal of Political and Military Sociology, 18*, 177–230.

Brown, E. (2014, August 14). Timeline: Michael Brown shooting in Ferguson, MO. *USA Today*. Retrieved from www.usatoday.com/story/news/nation/2014/08/14/michael-brown-ferguson-missouri-timeline/14051827/

Brown, M., Ray, R., Summers, E., & Fraistat, N. (2017). #SayHerName: A case study of intersectional social media activism. *Ethnic and Racial Studies, 40*(11), 1831–1846. doi: 10.1080/01419870.2017.1334934

Chappell, B. (2018, May 4). College apologizes after Native American students' visit is sidelined by police. *National Public Radio*. Retrieved from www.npr.org/sections/thetwo-way/2018/05/04/608533284/college-apologizes-after-native-american-students-visit-is-sidelined-by-police

Cho, K. S. (2018). The perception of progress: Conceptualizing institutional response to student protests and activism. *Thought & Action, 34*(1), 81–95.

Chronicle of Higher Education (n.d.). *Title IX: Tracking sexual assault investigations*. Retrieved from https://projects.chronicle.com/titleix/

Chung, M., & Payne, A. (2015, November 11). Inspired by Mizzou protests, students across country focus on being #BlackonCampus. *NBC News*. Retrieved from www.nbcnews.com/news/nbcblk/inspired-mizzou-protests-ithaca-students-rally-demand-resignation-n461646

Clawson, J. (2014). Coming out of the classroom closet: The emerging visibility of queer students at the University of Florida, 1970–1982. *Educational Studies: A Journal of the American Educational Studies Association, 50*(3), 209–230.

Cohen, R. (2013). *Rebellion in black and white: Southern student activism in the 1960s*. Baltimore, MD: The John Hopkins University Press.

Cohen, A. M., & Kisker, C. B. (2010). *The shaping of American higher education: Emergence and growth of the contemporary system*. San Francisco, CA: Jossey-Bass.

Cole, E. R. (2018). College presidents and black student protests: A historical perspective on the image of racial inclusion and the reality of exclusion. *Peabody Journal of Education, 93*(1), 78–89. doi:10.1080/0161956X.2017.1403180

Crawford, H. E. (2015, November 9). *How long was Jonathan Butler's hunger strike? The university of Missouri student made a pledge & stuck to it*. Retrieved from www.bustle.com/articles/122540-how-long-was-jonathan-butlers-hunger-strike-the-university-of-missouri-student-made-a-pledge

[CTV 11]. (2015, November 17). *CSU Solidarity with Mizzou Protests* [Video file]. Retrieved from www.youtube.com/watch?v=OtPjCMQHwgM

Dansforth, S. (2018). Becoming the rolling quads: Disability politics at the university of California, Berkeley, in the 1960s. *History of Education Quarterly, 58*(4), 506–536. doi:10.1017/heq.2018.29

DeAngelo, L., Schuster, M. T., & Stebleton, M. J. (2016). California dreamers: Activism, identity, and empowerment among undocumented college students. *Journal of Diversity in Higher Education, 9*(3), 216–230.

Delgado Bernal, D. (1998). Grassroots leadership reconceptualized: Chicana oral histories and the 1968 East Los Angeles School blowouts. *Frontiers, 19*(2), 113–142.

Dargis, M. (2015, February 26). Review: "The Hunting Ground" documentary, a searing look at campus rape. *The New York Times*. Retrieved from www.nytimes.com/2015/02/27/movies/review-the-hunting-ground-documentary-a-searing-look-at-campus-rape.html

Dixson, A. D. (2018). "What's going on?": A critical race theory perspective on black lives matter and activism in education. *Urban Education, 53*(2), 231–247. doi:10.1177/0042085917747115

Dominguez, R. F. (2009). U.S. college student activism during an era of neoliberalism: A qualitative study of students against sweatshops. *The Australian Educational Researcher, 36*(3), 125–138.

Dorn, C. (2017). *For the common good: A new history of higher education in America*. Ithaca, NY: Cornell University Press.

End Rape on Campus. (n.d.). *Frequently asked questions*. Retrieved from https://endrapeoncampus.org/faq

Fain, P. (2017, January 30). Forceful response. *Inside Higher Ed*. Retrieved from www.insidehighered.com/news/2017/01/30/higher-education-leaders-denounce-trumps-travel-ban

Ferguson, R. A. (2019). *One-dimensional queer*. Medford, MA: Polity Press.

Filby, M. (2016, December 5). UD students sleep out to show support for pipeline protest. *Dayton Daily News*. Retrieved from www.daytondailynews.com/news/local/students-sleep-out-show-support-for-pipeline-protest/pb0buhzZvWqOjrBoiz6emM/

Flaherty, C. (2017, December 8). "Holding space" for victims of harassment. *Inside Higher Ed*. Retrieved from www.insidehighered.com/news/2017/12/08/what-can-crowdsourced-survey-sexual-harassment-academia-tell-us-about-problem

Flaherty, C. (2018, September 20). Beyond naming to shame. *Inside Higher Ed*. Retrieved from www.insidehighered.com/news/2018/09/20/why-one-academic-spends-hours-week-putting-together-spreadsheet-documented

Frej, W. (2014, August 29). "*I just want my campus back*". Retrieved from www.msnbc.com/ronan-farrow-daily/i-just-want-my-campus-back

Gambino, L., Siddiqui, S., Owen, P., & Helmore, E. (2017, January 29). Thousands protest against Trump travel ban in cities and airports nationwide. *The Guardian*. Retrieved from www.theguardian.com/us-news/2017/jan/29/protest-trump-travel-ban-muslims-airports

Gaston-Gayles, J. L., Wolf-Wendel, L. E., Tuttle, K. N., Twombly, S. B., & Ward, K. (2005). From disciplinarian to change agent: How the civil rights era changed the roles of student affairs professionals. *NASPA Journal, 42*(3), 263–282.

Goodman, J. (2016). *UR students protest dakota access pipeline, support standing Rock Sioux.* Retrieved from www.democratandchronicle.com/story/news/2016/11/15/ur-students-protest-dakota-pipeline-launch-ur-fossil-free-campaign/93801284/

Goyette, B., & Rothberg, P. (2011, January 15). *The top 14 student activism stories of the year.* Retrieved from www.thenation.com/article/top-14-student-activism-stories-year/

Greenlaw, M. (2017, December 24). *The Oscar Grant (Oakland) Protests, 2009–2011.* Retrieved from www.blackpast.org/aaw/oscar-grant-oakland-protests-2009-2011/

Griffin, T. (2015, November 7). How Sandra Bland's historical black college town is—and isn't—remembering her. *Buzzfeed News.* Retrieved from www.buzzfeednews.com/article/tamerragriffin/sandra-bland-prairie-view

Hall, R. M., & Sandler, B. R. (1982). *The campus climate: Report of the project on the status and education of women.* Washington, DC: Association of American Colleges.

Harrison, L. M. (2010). Consequences and strategies student affairs professionals engage in their advocacy roles. *Journal of Student Affairs Research and Practice, 47*(2), 197–214.

Harrison, L. M. (2014). How student affairs professionals learn to advocate: A phenomenological study. *Journal of College and Character, 15*(3), 165–178. doi:10.1515/jcc-2014–0020

Harrison, L. M., & Mather, P. C. (2017). Making meaning of student activism: Student activist and administrator perspectives. *Mid-Western Educational Researcher, 29*(2), 117–135.

Heineck, K. (2012, March 27). *Virginia tech students hold "hoodie March" for Trayvon Martin.* Retrieved from www.dailyprogress.com/newsvirginian/news/virginia-tech-students-hold-hoodie-march-for-trayvon-martin/article_4af1d752-1e34-592d-b85a-edf87bbee1e0.html

Hersher, R. (2017, February 22). Key moments in the Dakota Access Pipeline fight. *NPR.* Retrieved from www.npr.org/sections/thetwo-way/2017/02/22/514988040/key-moments-in-the-dakota-access-pipeline-fight

Hine, D. C. (1996). The Kent State Era, 1968–1970: Legacies of student rebellion and state repression. *Peace & Change, 21*(2), 157–168.

Holston, P. (2016, August 11). *Experts say white supremacists see Trump as 'last stand'.* Retrieved from www.pbs.org/newshour/politics/experts-say-white-supremacists-see-trump-last-stand

Hope, E. C., Keels, M., & Durkee, M. I. (2016). Participation in black lives matter and deferred action for childhood arrivals: Modern activism among Black and Latino college students. *Journal of Diversity in Higher Education, 9*(3), 203–215.

Izadi, E. (2015, November 9). The incidents that led to the university of Missouri president's resignation. *The Washington Post.* Retrieved from www.washingtonpost.com/news/grade-point/wp/2015/11/09/the-incidents-that-led-to-the-university-of-missouri-presidents-resignation/

Jarrett, L., & Tatum, S. (2017, September 25). Trump administration announces new travel restrictions. *CNN.* Retrieved from www.cnn.com/2017/09/24/politics/trump-travel-restrictions/index.html

Jaschik, S. (2016, November 10). Outraged by Trump win, students protest. *Inside Higher Ed.* Retrieved from www.insidehighered.com/news/2016/11/10/numerous-campuses-see-protests-students-react-shock-trump-victory

Katznelson, I. (2005). *When affirmative action was white: An untold history of racial inequality in twentieth-century America.* New York, NY: W. W. Norton & Company, Inc.

Kendi, I. X. (2013). *The black campus movement: Black students and the racial reconstitution of higher education, 1965–1972.* New York, NY: Palgrave Macmillan.

Kezar, A. (2010). Faculty and staff partnering with student activists: Unexplored terrains of interaction and development. *Journal of College Student Development, 51*(5), 451–480.

Kilgallen, M. (2017, February 1). *Stony Brook community denounces travel ban at two separate protests*. Retrieved from www.sbstatesman.com/2017/02/01/stony-brook-community-denounces-travel-ban-at-two-separate-protests/

Know Your IX. (n.d.). *Learn about Know Your IX*. Retrieved www.knowyourix.org/about/

Kramer, P. A. (2018, January 22). Trump's anti-immigration racism represents an American tradition. *The New York Times*. Retrieved from www.nytimes.com/2018/01/22/opinion/trumps-anti-immigrant-racism-represents-an-american-tradition.html

Labaree, D. F. (1997). Public goods, private goods: The American struggle over educational goals. *American Educational Research Journal, 34*(1), 39–81.

Levine, A., & Wilson, K. R. (1979). Student activism in the 1970s: Transformation not decline. *Higher Education, 8*(6), 627–640. Retrieved from www.jstor.org/stable/3446223

Linder, C. (2019). Power-conscious and intersectional approaches to supporting student activists: Considerations for learning and development. *Journal of Diversity in Higher Education, 12*(1), 17–26. http://dx.doi.org/10.1037/dhe0000082

Linder, C., Myers, J. S., Riggle, C., & Lacy, M. (2016). From margins to mainstream: Social media as a tool for campus sexual violence activism. *Journal of Diversity in Higher Education, 9*(3), 231–244. doi:10.1037/dhe0000038

Mangan, K. (2018, June 26). How a student used title IX to force her college to change her response to cases of sexual assault. *The Chronicle of Higher Education*. Retrieved from www.chronicle.com/article/How-a-Student-Used-Title-IX-to/243763

Marine, S. B., & Nicolazzo, Z. (2014). Names that matter: Exploring the tensions of campus LGBTQ centers and trans* inclusion. *Journal of Diversity in Higher Education, 7*(4), 265–281.

Mathias, C. (2013, March 12). Flatbush riot: Vigil for Kimani Gray, 16-year-old shot and killed by NYPD cops, turns violent (Photos). *Huffington Post*. Retrieved from www.huffingtonpost.com/2013/03/12/flatbush-riot-kimani-gray-vigil-killed-by-nypd-cops-violent_n_2857716.html

Maxwell, A. (2016, July 7). How Southern racism found a home in the tea party. *Vox*. Retrieved from www.vox.com/2016/7/7/12118872/southern-racism-tea-party-trump

McElderry, J. A., & Hernandez Rivera, S. (2017). "Your agenda item, our experience": Two administrators' insights on campus unrest at Mizzou. *The Journal of Negro Education, 86*(3), 318–337.

McGuire, D. L. (2010). *At the dark end of the street: Black women, rape, and resistance: A new history of the civil rights movement from Rosa Parks to the rise of black power*. New York, NY: Alfred A. Knopf.

McMahon, J. (2016, November 16). *1,000 students declare Syracuse university, SUNY ESF a 'sanctuary campus'*. Retrieved from www.syracuse.com/su-news/2016/11/1000_students_declare_syracuse.html

Moore, K. M. (1997). Freedom and constraint in eighteenth century Harvard. In L. F. Goodchild, & H. Weschler (Eds.), *The history of higher education* (2nd ed., pp. 108–114). Needham Heights, MA: Simon and Schuster.

Muñoz, S. M. (2015). *Identity, activism, and the pursuit of higher education: The journey stories of undocumented and unafraid community activists*. New York, NY: Peter Lange Publishing, Inc.

Nash, M. A., & Silverman, J. A. R. (2015). "An indelible mark": Gay purges in higher education in the 1940s. *History of Education Quarterly, 55*(4), 441–459.

Nguyen, T., & Gasman, M. (2015). Activism, identity and service: The influence of the Asian American movement on the educational experiences of college students. *History of Education, 44*(3), 339–354. doi:10.1080/0046760X.2014.1003338

Park, H., & Lee, J. C. (2017, May 3). *Looking for accountability in police-involved deaths of Blacks*. Retrieved from www.nytimes.com/interactive/2016/07/12/us/looking-for-accountability-in-police-involved-deaths-of-blacks.html

Patton Davis, L. (2010). *Culture centers in higher education: Perspectives on identity, theory, and practice*. Sterling, VA: Stylus Press.

Patton Davis, L. (2015, November 16). Why have the demands of Black students changed so little since the 1960s. *The Conversation*. Retrieved from http://theconversation.com/why-have-the-demands-of-black-students-changed-so-little-since-the-1960s-50695

Pauker, M. (2016, November 10). Students protest election with 'Love Trumps Hate Rally' on campus. *Daily Bruin*. Retrieved from http://dailybruin.com/2016/11/10/students-protest-election-with-love-trumps-hate-rally-on-campus/

Pisner, N. (2011, October 20). Past tense: A tradition of protest. *The Crimson*. Retrieved from www.thecrimson.com/article/2011/10/20/city-protests-history/

Pratt, R. A. (2002). *We shall not be moved: The desegregation of the University of Georgia*. Athens, GA: University of Georgia Press.

Quaye, S. J., Shaw, M. D., & Hill, D. C. (2017). Blending scholar and activist identities: Establishing the need for scholar activism. *Journal of Diversity in Higher Education, 10*(4), 381–399.

Raghunathan, S. (2017, September 11). Too many Americans think patriotism means racism and xenophobia. *The Nation*. Retrieved from www.thenation.com/article/too-many-americans-think-patriotism-means-racism-and-xenophobia/

Reich, G., & Barth, J. (2010). Educating citizens or defying federal authority? A comparative study of in-state tuition for undocumented students. *The Policy Studies Journal, 38*(3), 419–445.

Reichard, D. A. (2010). 'We can't hide and they are wrong': The society for homosexual freedom and the struggle for recognition at Sacramento State College, 1969–1971. *Law and History Review, 28*(3), 629–674.

Robertson, L. (2018, January 22). The facts on DACA. *Factcheck.org*. Retrieved from www.factcheck.org/2018/01/the-facts-on-daca/

Rosenblum, M. R. (2011). *US immigration policy since 9/11: Understanding the stalemate over comprehensive immigration reform*. Washington, DC: Migration Policy Institute.

Rhoads, R. A. (1998). Student protest and multicultural reform: Making sense of campus unrest in the 1990s. *The Journal of Higher Education, 69*(6), 621–646. doi:10.2307/2649211

Rhoads, R. A. (2016). Student activism, diversity, and the struggle for a just society. *Journal of Diversity in Higher Education, 9*(3), 189–202.

Reuben, M. A. (1998). Reforming the university: Student protests and the demand for a 'relevant' curriculum. In G. De Groot (Ed.), *Student protest: The sixties and after* (pp. 153–168). New York, NY: Longman.

Scott, E. (2018, October 8). President Trump, 'angry mobs' and 'very fine people'. *The Washington Post*. Retrieved from www.washingtonpost.com/politics/2018/10/08/president-trump-angry-mobs-very-fine-people/

Slevin, P. (2010, July 26). Deportation of illegal immigrants increases under Obama administration. *The Washington Post*. Retrieved from www.washingtonpost.com/wp-dyn/content/article/2010/07/25/AR2010072501790.html?hpid=topnews

Solomon, B. M. (1985). *In the company of educated women*. New Haven, CT: Yale University Press.

Stewart, D. L. (2011). *Multicultural student services on campus: Building bridges, revisioning community*. Sterling, VA: Stylus.

Stewart, T. J., & Quaye, S. J. (2019). Building bridges: Rethinking student activist leadership. In G. Martin, C. Linder, & B. M. Williams (Eds.), *Leadership learning through activism: New directions for student leadership, 160*. San Francisco, CA: Wiley.

Stirgus, E. (2018, August 7). Professor says Georgia college had him sign pledge saying he isn't a communist party member. *Atlanta Journal Constitution*. Retrieved from www.ajc.com/news/local-education/professor-says-georgia-college-had-him-sign-pledge-saying-isn-communist/ZukaGj9SNY8OllJvNfJdKP/

Subramaniam, A. (2016, November 11). Hundreds of Cornellians walk out of class, protesting election's 'hate speech'. *Cornell Sun*. Retrieved from https://cornellsun.com/tag/the-peoples-walkout/

Svokos, A. (2014, October 29). Students bring out mattresses in huge 'Carry that weight' protest against sexual assault. *Huffington Post*. Retrieved from www.huffingtonpost.com/2014/10/29/carry-that-weight-columbia-sexual-assault_n_6069344.html

Swem, L. L. (1987). Due process rights in student disciplinary matters. *Journal of College and University Law, 14*, 359–382.

Taha, D., Hastings, S. O., & Minei, E. M. (2015). Shaping student activists: Discursive sensemaking of activism and participation research. *Journal of the Scholarship of Teaching and Learning, 15*(6), 1–15. doi: https://doi.org/10.14434/josotl.v15i6.13820

Thelin, J. R. (2011). *A history of American higher education* (2nd ed.). Baltimore, MD: The Johns Hopkins University Press.

Thornhill, T. (2018). We want black students, just not you: How white admissions counselors screen black prospective students. *Sociology of Race and Ethnicity*. Online first, https://doi.org/10.1177/2332649218792579

Whaley, N. (2016, August 3). Why we can't keep forgetting Black women are being harmed by police violence too. *VH1 News*. Retrieved from www.vh1.com/news/275984/black-women-police-violence/

Wilder, C. S. (2013). *Ebony & ivy: Race, slavery, and the troubled history of America's universities*. New York, NY: Bloomsbury Press.

Williamson, J. A. (2003). *Black power on campus: The university of Illinois, 1965–75*. Urbana, IL: University of Illinois Press.

Williamson-Lott, J. A. (2018). *Jim Crow campus: Higher education and the struggle for a new Southern social order*. New York, NY: Teachers College Press.

Winston, F. (2013). Decisions to make a difference: The role of efficacy in moderate student activism. *Social Movement Studies: Journal of Social, Cultural and Political Protest, 12*(4), 414–428.

Wolf-Wendel, L., Twombly, S. B., Tuttle, K. N., Ward, K., & Gaston-Gayles, J. L. (2004). Reflecting back: Themes from the cases. In *Reflecting back, looking forward: Civil rights and student affairs* (pp. 321–372). Washington, DC: NASPA.

Wright, B. (1988). For the children of the infidels? American Indian education in the colonial colleges. *American Indian Culture and Research Journal, 12*(3), 1–14.

Ye He Lee, M. (2015 July 8). Donald Trump's false comments connecting Mexican immigrants and crime. *The Washington Post*. Retrieved from www.washingtonpost.com/news/fact-checker/wp/2015/07/08/donald-trumps-false-comments-connecting-mexican-immigrants-and-crime/?utm_term=.92e20c87650b

3

SITUATING THE STUDY OF IDENTITY-BASED ACTIVISM ON U.S. COLLEGE CAMPUSES

From our collective academic and practitioner experiences, specifically as people who have great interest in equity and justice on college campuses, we know that power and dominance manifest and are reproduced on/in college campus environments. Further, we understand the past informs the present as it relates to the contexts students maneuver in and through their activism. As Ferguson (2017) points out when writing to student activists,

> For all their seeming newness, our present-day troubles are not entirely different from the ones that previous students struggled over. Like everything "new" they have part of their genesis in "bygone" battles. In other words, there's much we can learn from those earlier campaigns as we figure out how to clarify and launch our own.
>
> *(p. 4)*

Indeed, the struggles of students are linked to a history of struggle in the United States that dates back to settler colonialism and the transatlantic slave trade and are direct manifestations of power and dominance (Rogers, 2012; Sui, 2015). These historic struggles continue to inform how power manifests and materializes on college campuses today.

Campus politics contextualize how and why college students engage in activism. Often student activists' decision to engage reflects campus leaders' failure to adequately respond to or provide support for students' negative experiences. Minoritized students, often turned student activists, experience numerous forms of systematic oppression, including, but not limited to, classism, transphobia, xenophobia, homophobia, sexism, and racism, as indicated by participant stories in later chapters. When students raise their voices in an attempt to illuminate harmful campus cultures, institutional leaders sometimes view them as problems on campus and disruptive to normal campus life (Martin, 2014; Linder, Quaye, Stewart, Okello, & Roberts, 2017; Spade, 2017).

In this chapter, we focus on outlining key concepts that inform current contexts for identity-based activism and subsequent chapters in this text. Consider this chapter an invitation to the ideas, concepts, and constructs that we explored, examined, and discussed to edify our understanding of student activist stories. First, we briefly discuss and situate activism and resistance and the types of activities and engagement in which participants engaged as student activists. Next, we situate the concept of labor (both physical and emotional) within the context of student activism. Then, we briefly discuss institutional betrayal and situate institutional leaders as violating student trust when they fail to adequately respond to student concerns. After that, we outline the concept of neoliberalism and connections we perceive to identity-based college student activism. Finally, we examine the role of educators and identity-based student activism by reviewing current literature of activism and relationships of student activists and the educators who are supposed to support them.

Activism and Resistance

Activism and resistance, two likely familiar terms, are often (mis)understood and conflated in public discourse. Typically, activism is considered traditional, public, and visual acts of disruption or advocacy toward making social change, including marches, protests, sit-ins, and petitions (Johansson & Vinthagen, 2016). However, those public acts are often named as resistance, and resistance is sometimes problematically reduced to *only* those acts. While traditional displays of activism *can* be resistance, as all activism is resistance, not all resistance is activism (Stewart & Williams, in press). Resistance includes "actions that have the potential to undermine power but can also function as part of everyday life" (Stewart & Williams, in press). For example, when asked about her activism, Averi, a white, queer/asexual, non-able bodied, and agender person, stated the following,

> Within clinical trainings I try to teach [clinicians] how to work around [client social] identities without making [social] identity the problem. With clients, I try helping clients that are usually hurt historically by clinicians to understand their rights are. Whenever I start working with any client, I tell them if they don't feel okay with what I'm doing to tell me. If they don't feel they are okay to tell me, they can tell another therapist that they have and what kind of steps they can go through. That way, it's not just the clinician as the expert and they do what they do, and I [the client] have to succumb to that. I also try within classroom teaching. There [in the classroom] I usually try to have my syllabus reflective of those not normally in it. I have

> very specific examples, very specific videos. I try and talk about how things have come to be, rather than just where they are.

Some might struggle to see how Averi's work meets prevailing definitions of activism. She intentionally trains ethical and power-conscious clinicians and deliberately crafts her classroom spaces, as a doctoral-level instructor, to reflect the people, communities, and voices often left out of the academic discourses. Although in this example, Averi does not describe protesting or marching, she demonstrates a clear commitment to justice and equity and identifies herself as an activist. Averi's resistance of dominant ways of teaching and training clinicians represents a form of activism frequently ignored in public discourse about activism.

When thinking about activism, and specifically resistance, it may be helpful to try and distinguish the purpose or intent of participants' action and the methods they employ to achieve that intent or purpose, as the combination of both informs the resistance or activism more clearly (Stewart & Williams, in press). For example, Ghassan, a Muslim Palestinian American man, shared,

> My definition of activism is generally spread[ing] awareness about a specific cause or happening in the world, be it local or global. The term organizing has more to do with actual actions to complement the activism. But activism is about raising awareness about a specific cause or injustice and through that awareness, try and incite a sort of demand for political change.

Based on Ghassan's definition, activism is more about the purpose/intent of any given action and not necessarily the means. A person could engage in a march, protest, sit-in, digital/hashtag campaign, or a teach-in and be considered engaging in activism through raising awareness. Further, for Ghassan, while connected to activism, organizing is also slightly different than being an activist, as activism is about raising awareness and organizing is about the specific actions to create change based on the awareness raised by the activism. These descriptions by Averi, Ghassan, and other participants point to the complexity of terminology between activism, resistance, organizing, and mobilizing for college student activists. In fact, despite participation of students with minoritized identities in this study about "student activists," many students do not identify with the term *activist* and consider their existence as a form of resistance in hostile campus environments (Stewart, in press; Linder et al., 2017).

In the next several chapters, we present more about participants' experiences and interests as they relate to their activist work. They engage in traditional forms of activism, advocacy, and protest, yet they also situate their teaching in the classroom, participation as students in the classroom, leadership roles in student organizations, and work in the community as types of activism and/or resistance. Throughout this book, we portray the complexity of these concepts when engaging participants' stories and experiences as we collectively work to understand what activism and resistance mean to them, what counts as activism and resistance, and the broad variance of action that make up their collective efforts for equity and justice on their campuses.

Labor

The concept of labor is intrinsically connected to important histories in the United States. From the labor forced upon enslaved Africans as a result of the transatlantic slave trade, to the history of blue-collar workers and their fight for labor unions, to Black women mobilizing to have their labor recognized and paid for, as well as their advocacy for better labor conditions, labor is intrinsically tied to power. Later, we discuss identity-based student activism in a labor context and discuss our framing for that context here. First, we highlight work on gender and emotional labor to articulate the particular ways labor is gendered and the implications of understanding labor in this way. We then examine the connection between racial battle fatigue, white fragility, and emotional labor in order to illustrate the particular ways People of Color engage in labor as a result of their interactions with white people.

Gender and Emotional Labor

Stemming from studies of gender dynamics in workplaces (Pierce, 1996), the term emotional labor describes the energy and time women spend managing their emotions in the workplace, so as to not upset men. This management of emotions leads women to experience isolation, shaming, and toxicity in work environments (Evans & Moore, 2015). Even though men can freely express strong feelings such as anger, without fear of retribution, women must manage those same feelings so as to not be described as unprofessional or overly sensitive by men (Evans & Moore, 2015). In workplaces, men can spend their energy on completing the demands of work, which has professional benefits, such as higher pay and career advancement. Women, on the other hand, must spend an inordinate amount of their energy on managing men's feelings and working to illustrate that they are equally competent. This additional labor takes time away from them being able to spend their energy on the same tasks as men, which in turn, has consequences in their pay and career advancement (Evans & Moore, 2015).

In addition to the ivory tower articulations of the term emotional labor, many organizers, artists, and writers have begun to situate emotional labor in new and nuanced contexts. For example, in digital spaces (such as Twitter), Black women have situated the concept of labor to include the work that people with minoritized identities often perform to educate and inform those with dominant identities or labor where there is a strenuous and personal emotional connection/impact to the person engaging the labor (Carruthers, 2015; Threads of Solidarity, 2018; Trudy, 2013). Not only are these examples of labor, but they are also examples of *unpaid* labor and a new(er) articulation of emotional labor because of the stress and duress endured and experienced by the minoritized people when trying to defend themselves and their positions, as well as teaching others what it means to be them in the world. For example, Amari Gaiter (2018), a Black woman undergraduate student wrote the following in her op-ed titled "Black Emotional Labor Is Core to My Columbia Experience,"

> I did not realize that in addition to mandatory coursework and rigorous academics, I would frequently be required to offer my existence and knowledge as learning tools, let others challenge the fabric of my humanity, and allow my peers to use my emotional vulnerabilities for the greater sake of education and awareness. I am never thanked for my emotional expenditures, but I am always left feeling as if I've made a slight impact on my counterparts' thinking and worldview, and by extension made the world a slightly better place. Thus, I am left with a conflict: Do I self-sacrifice for the greater good of our community, or prioritize my own well-being? Society chooses for me, and I am left as the instructor of an additional course titled "Free Black Emotional Labor."
>
> *(para 1)*

Gaiter's articulation, and that of many other minoritized people—specifically Black women and femmes—seems to be more in line with the experiences of activists in this study and the stories that they share. This reality should be unsurprising given that they constantly have to fight and advocate for their needs in order to be treated equitably at their institutions.

Racial Battle Fatigue and White Fragility as Emotional Labor

Racial battle fatigue describes the exhaustion that People of Color feel from continued exposure to racial microaggressions and racism (Smith, Allen, & Danley, 2007). Racial microaggressions consist of small, seemingly innocuous insults that accumulate over time (Sue, 2010); microaggressions contribute to People of Color experiencing racial battle fatigue. A security officer following a Person of Color in a store, telling someone with an accent that they speak English really well, or willfully touching a Black woman's hair without permission constitute examples of racial microaggressions. When a Person of Color shares their frustration and boundaries, the perpetrator of the microaggression often indicates that they did not mean their actions, which further exacerbates the racial battle fatigue. People of Color are tired from experiencing racism; however, even more significant are the emotional, mental, and physical costs of racial battle fatigue (Quaye, Carter, Allen, Karikari, & Okello, 2018). Continued exposure to racism has deleterious consequences on the health and well-being of People of Color (Arnold, Crawford, & Khalifa, 2016), leading to higher blood pressure, anxiety, sleeplessness, diabetes, and shortened lifespan (Arnold et al., 2016; Gorski, 2019; Smith et al., 2007).

People of Color also must manage their emotions as they experience racism in the presence of white people, which is a form of extra labor they perform. When People of Color, for example, point out racial microaggressions or overt racism, white people often become defensive or resistant, or they minimize that racism (DiAngelo, 2011). These feelings of defensiveness and resistance are associated with white fragility, a concept that describes the lack of experience white people have in handling racial matters (DiAngelo, 2011). This lack of experience makes them fragile when engaged in conversations about race and racism and uncertain of how to respond. Each of these actions (e.g., defensiveness, resistance, shutting down, minimization) works to center whiteness and white fragility, thereby putting the responsibility onto People of Color for managing white people's feelings and emotions.

As such, People of Color often spend an inordinate amount of time figuring out how to navigate predominantly white spaces in order to protect white people's feelings, often to the detriment of their own well-being. As one can imagine, this management of white people's reactions and feelings exhausts People of Color and takes time away from them putting their energy into more life-giving activities, such as centering their own self-care and healing processes (Quaye, Karikari, Allen, Okello, & Carter, 2018). By naming and addressing racism, People of Color risk further isolating themselves and having to manage white people's feelings, as well as negative consequences in the workplace. However, by not naming racism, their silence further harms them by suffering their trauma in isolation without possibilities to address the harm (Evans & Moore, 2015).

In Chapter 5, we share student activists' experiences with and the costs of their unpaid and emotional labor, as well as the corresponding stress and trauma of engaging in the labor of making their campuses better. To be sure, student activism is certainly physical: students organize, mobilize, march, demonstrate; they move about and throughout the campus to raise awareness. Their activism is also deeply emotional and connected to their identities and personhood; as such, it affects them deeply in their daily lives. Student activists in this book also highlight their experiences with gaslighting and being placated by campus administrators (Chapter 6), their experiences being surveilled on campus (Chapter 5), and how all of these experiences negatively impact their energy, well-being, and feelings of safety at their institutions (Chapters 4, 5, & 6). Students advocate for themselves; manage their own feelings; and manage dominance in the forms of whiteness, heteronormativity, and American imperialism, all while trying to care for themselves. Indeed, activists articulate the cost of their labor and the gravity of the laborious conditions they maneuver. Student activists also manage the impact of institutional betrayal on their everyday lived experiences. Institutional betrayal also becomes a motivator for many student activists to engage in resistance and organizing on their campuses.

Institutional Betrayal

The concept of institutional betrayal has origins in betrayal trauma theory, which posits that abuse perpetrated within close relationships is more harmful than abuse perpetrated by strangers (Freyd, 1996). Institutional betrayal occurs when institutions or organizations perpetuate or remain ignorant to instances of trauma experienced by members of their community (Smith & Freyd, 2014). Institutions that "foster a sense of trust or dependency" (Smith & Freyd, 2014, p. 578) may perpetuate institutional betrayal by violating that sense of trust and dependency. Institutional leaders may commit betrayal through acts of commission or omission, which means any member of an organization may commit institutional betrayal without the awareness of doing so (Smith & Freyd, 2014).

Tenets of institutional betrayal include failing to prevent harm, normalizing harmful contexts, creating difficult processes for reporting harm, failing to adequately respond to instances of harm, supporting cover-ups and misinformation, and punishing victims and whistleblowers (Smith & Freyd, 2014). Although Smith and Freyd's (2014) theory originated out of work related to sexual violence, institutional betrayal may occur related to other instances of harm experienced by members of a community, especially harm related to power differentials within an environment (Smith & Freyd, 2013). For example, when students experience racism, sexism, ableism, homophobia, or transphobia and the institution fails to respond appropriately, institutional betrayal occurs. Some students report that their experiences with the lack of institutional response to the harm they experienced is more significant than the original harm (Linder & Myers, 2017).

One of the key assumptions of institutional betrayal includes a sense of trust or dependency on the organization perpetuating the betrayal. The notion of trust between students with minoritized identities and the institutions they attend is complex. Based on previous experiences with racism, homophobia, and other forms of oppression, some minoritized students have likely learned not to trust most "institutions," including institutions of higher education. However, minoritized students may have an expectation of physical and mental safety—even if implicit—based on institutional promises. Colleges and universities often feature minoritized students in their recruitment brochures, on websites, during campus tours, and during orientation (Pippert, Essenburg, & Matchett, 2013). As we discuss later, college students engaged in identity-based student activism sometimes find the promises of their institutions (e.g., safety, success, community, and equitable support/opportunity) do not materialize for them.

Further, even when students do not have explicit trust in the institution, they are likely still dependent on the institution for a variety of things. Minoritized students, like the students in our study, likely attend college as a means to survive and thrive in the world (Huerta, McDonough, & Allen, 2018) and intrinsically have some level of dependency on their institutions (e.g., using scholarship and loan money for living expenses, needing sponsorship for student visas, having access to employment and campus resources solely because of a student designation) so they can matriculate and graduate. Further, if a student finds that a particular institution is challenging to their lives and personhood, it is difficult to transfer to another institution, which may result in students deciding to stay at their institutions and try to make them better, rather than moving and hoping a new institution is affirming to their identities and lives. Finally, some minoritized students have a genuine love of or loyalty to their institution and want it to be better for the students who come after them.

In Chapter 4, we cite anger as a motivation for some students' activism. While students may not use the term *institutional betrayal* to describe how and why their anger materialized, they articulate a reality that a) they are often harmed by their institutions and b) when they vocalize that harm, institutional leaders fail to respond and provide support, which is illustrative of the concept of institutional betrayal. They find their lives, personhood, and experiences under surveillance, scrutiny, and attack (Chapters 4 and 5), and as a result, they experience betrayal because they either had trust that institutional leaders would support their success and well-being, or they find themselves at the mercy of their institutions to survive regardless of the trust they may or may not have.

Neoliberalism

Neoliberalism is a confusing term that can have both no real meaning and an infinite number of meanings (Rodgers, 2018). In 2009, a pair of researchers reviewed 148 articles on neoliberalism and argued that social science researchers invoke the term *neoliberalism* in ways that obscure an already ambiguous term. Social scientists frequently use the term to articulate the belief that an unregulated business/consumer market increases social good (Boas & Gans-Morse 2009). For the purposes of this text, when we refer to neoliberalism, we mean "a model of capitalism that operates through the privatization of public goods, deregulation of trade, diminishment of social services, and emphasis on individual freedoms" (Carruthers, 2018, p. x), a definition that has strong connections to higher education.

Historically, public discourses about liberalism, informed by legislators and corporations, have been framed to working-class and poor people as a more progressive alternative to conservative ideologies. However, while conservative politicians are ideologically at odds with "liberals," economic liberalism is quite beneficial to fiscal conservatives (Martinez & Garcia, 1997). Scholars describe the differences between liberalism and neoliberalism as follows,

> Liberalism is more a political philosophy that holds liberty to a high standard. It defines all social, economic, and political aspects of society, such as the role of government, toleration, freedom to act, etc. Conversely, neoliberalism focuses more on the markets, meaning it supports deregulation, ending protectionism, and freeing up the markets. Therefore, it is based on economics.
> *(Kenton, 2018, para 6)*

In this way, neoliberalism is not necessarily a new liberalism as much as it is a revival of a conservative economic ideology.

The Effects of Neoliberalism on Higher Education

To understand why neoliberalism has impacted higher education, we must trace the origins of higher education and its purported purpose. In 1862, President Lincoln signed the Morrill Act into law, which granted land to several states with a mission to make college accessible to the country's citizenry (Cohen & Kisker, 2010), although it is clear legislators did not mean *all* citizens, as institutions focused on supporting Black Americans did not receive federal support until the authorization of the second Morrill Act in 1890 (Cohen & Kisker, 2010). At the time, U.S. legislators held the prevalent idea that "knowledge, being necessary to good government and the happiness of mankind, schools and the means of education shall forever be encouraged" (Northwest Ordinance, 1787, Art. 3). This articulation is connected to a widely held understanding that the purpose of colleges and universities was to create informed citizens; that is, higher education is or should be a public good. During the Ronald Reagan era, that ideology began to shift; many politicians and people in the general public began to view higher education as non-essential, and as such, not a public good (Berrett, 2016). States received decreased funding and resources, and in turn, institutional leaders became driven to generate resources, seemingly above all else.

As neoliberalism swept the global economy, so too did it sweep institutions of higher education. The rise of terms such as *academic capitalism* and *the corporate university* (Seal, 2018) in the discourse point specifically to the way higher education has changed within a deep neoliberal context:

> Higher education was being "corporatized." Business values were seeping in to seminars. Students were learning to evaluate their course schedule like a bond trader looking over a portfolio, and they were being taught to do so not by their professors but by an exterior culture that sang the hymns of return on investment.
>
> *(Seal, 2018, para 8)*

Given these changes, higher education has become—perhaps more so than previously in its history—tied to the market and the behaviors thereof. Further, the tie of higher education to the market has resulted in colleges and universities structuring themselves on the basis of business principles and revenue generation (Saunders, 2007), as opposed to the needs of students or desirable outcomes for the public good. For example, the rise of for-profits, increased focus on research grants, reliance on contingent faculty, and an increased focus on science, technology, engineering, and mathematics (STEM) fields (and less on humanities) are all connected to a rise in neoliberal ethics (Kezar, 2004).

Identity-Based Activism as Resistance Against Neoliberal Campus Cultures

Neoliberalism manifests in several ways in higher education; those manifestations, coupled with students' experiences with dominance, compel them to engage in activism on their campuses. Further, an examination of higher education and neoliberalism centering power and identity, educators "may understand student movements as efforts to illustrate the connections among systems of power that arose *between* academy, government, and corporation" (Ferguson, 2017, p. 68, emphasis added), neoliberalism functions to suppress our collective recognition and understanding of the complexities of oppression and power as *interlocking systems* that affect the lives of minoritized people both on and off campus (Ferguson, 2017).

College students engaging in activism could be considered as a form of resistance to neoliberalism broadly as well as a way forward, out of neoliberalism. "In thinking about a vision of a post-neoliberal or post-capitalist world, contemporary student activism and college student protesters' demands offer some inkling of what that might look like" (Cole & Heinecke, 2018, p. 3). Given this framing, student activists, as they work to resist oppressive structures, operate as a canary in the proverbial mine. That is, students demonstrating on their campuses illustrate that not only are campus contexts and conditions problematic and violent, but they are also symptomatic as they are born out of similar societal realities.

In Chapters 4–6, participants articulate ideas connected to neoliberalism within their colleges and universities. One participant discussed administrators who were fearful of losing money for the institution, and therefore, took apolitical stances to the issues identity-based student activists raised (Chapter 6). Lack of administrators' deliberate effort toward the issues and concerns of student activists, tied to a desire to remain neutral for monetary and political reasons, increased labor and stress on student activists (Chapter 5). Another participant named issues with legislative control over their campuses and how the decisions of the legislature added additional work for them by way of advocacy and activism on their campus (Chapter 4). Indeed, we perceived several connections to neoliberalism in higher education as evidenced by participant stories.

Role of Educators With Student Activists

Previous scholarship on student activism includes some attention to the role of educators working with student activists. Unfortunately, the majority of this scholarship approaches the topic from a power- and identity-neutral perspective, meaning that the researchers fail to account for the ways that identity and power influence students' relationships with educators. In Chapter 6, we examine these relationships more closely. In this section, we examine the literature about the role of educators with student activists, then highlight the significance of identity and power and its relationship to student activism.

The role of educators, including faculty, staff, and administrators, in working with student activists has been documented in the media and has begun to be explored in student affairs and higher education scholarship. Unfortunately, much of the scholarship about the role of educators in student activism fails to account for power as it relates to identity, meaning that the scholarship does not explore how consequences of supporting student activists are similar or different for educators with visible, salient minoritized identities and those with more dominant identities. Although some studies collected demographic information, noting the importance of the diversity of their samples, most researchers did not engage in analysis or discussion related to demographics (see Harrison, 2014; Kezar, 2010). However, Harrison (2010, 2014) examines the significance of hierarchical, institutional power in her research, providing some insight into the significance of power in educators' relationships to students and the institution. Given that power is inherently a part of relationships between students and educators, power should be a consideration in the research about the role of educators with student activism.

Some scholarship has examined the competing, sometimes conflicting, roles for educators seeking to work with student activists or engage in advocacy for students, including the role of power in this advocacy (Harrison, 2010, 2014). Student affairs educators report being poorly trained to engage in effective advocacy in the context of institutions with political and power dynamics related to money and policy (Harrison, 2014). Specifically, mid-level administrators feel pressure from students they work with to address institutional structures and policies that contribute to marginalization of students and pressure from senior administrators to uphold university policy (Harrison, 2010). Student affairs educators, especially those working in identity-based centers, reported experiencing significant consequences for advocating on behalf of students or not more effectively managing student unrest before it became a public issue for the institution. Consequences for challenging power included loss of "jobs, status, and morale" (Harrison, 2010, p. 208). Although Harrison (2010) did not specifically identify the identities of the participants to protect their confidentiality, one may assume that the staff in multicultural centers likely identified as People of Color and certainly experienced heightened scrutiny as a result of the political positions they were in.

Additional scholarship examines the ways students and educators interact related to student activism, yet the outcomes of this research differs, depending on a variety of factors, including the positionality of the participants in the studies and the perspective and frameworks employed by the researchers. For example, Kezar (2010) reports that faculty and staff often "partner" with students to disrupt institutional norms and cultures to enact change on campus (p. 451). The research points to important considerations in terms of institutional type, noting that students at liberal arts colleges tend to have more power than faculty and staff, while students at research institutions and community colleges tend to have less power.

Interestingly this study focuses on activism initiated by faculty and staff who seek out students to assist them in addressing their concerns. Kezar (2010) notes,

> Because faculty and staff are part of the institution, they risk their jobs if they push too hard for changes. Students are less at risk if they picket, contact the media, boycott, rally, or engage in other forms of overt activism. Strategically, faculty and staff partner with students who they know can take this more direct role when needed to create change. Also, when a topic gets too hot on the campus, students can maintain a leadership role when faculty and staff have to step aside.
>
> *(p. 470)*

Although the issues that faculty and staff seek to address may ultimately also benefit students, considering this finding through a power-conscious lens leads one to wonder which students "are less at risk" and what might happen if students approach faculty and staff with a concern or issue, rather than the other way around. Further, this type of method raises concerns and begs the question if partnering with students in the way described is a form of exploited student labor within campus movements spaces.

Similarly, Harrison and Mather (2017) selected three campuses to examine the ways students and administrators "made meaning of student activism" (p. 117), highlighting the significance of understanding the outcomes of student activism for both students and administrators. The researchers indicated that students and administrators experienced activism as "highly consequential" (Harrison & Mather, 2017, p. 126). Students indicated that they learned from their experiences as activists and appreciated being able to "apply what they were learning" (p. 129), and administrators experienced significant safety and legal concerns as a result of student activism. However, the researchers did not collect (or at least did not report) the social identities of their participants, leaving some questions as to what kind of learning happens and which students got to experience this learning. Were minoritized students equally as likely to experience learning as a result of their engagement with activism? Did administrators from minoritized social identities experience their work with student activists similarly as those with mostly dominant identities? Indeed, the relationships between student activist and the educators of their institutions are complex, and in Chapter 6 participants help demystify how relationships have materialized, or not, for them.

Conclusion

Each of the concepts considered in this chapter have connections to the experiences and stories of identity-based student activists. We deliberately centered identity and power in our inquiry, two concepts that are intertwined, much like the related concepts we have just outlined. In Part II of the book, student activists share in vivid detail their experiences working to dismantle oppression on their campuses. We invite you, the reader, to consider how neoliberalism might influence the issues and concerns they raise. Contemplate how their stories connect to physical and emotional labor, as well as emotional trauma. Reflect on the meaning of activism and resistance and the ways these students respond to betrayal by institutional leaders, who not only fail to protect them, but also do nothing when they are harmed. These concepts enrich the stories told and retold and will position the collective understanding of student activist experiences so that educators can do more to support them.

References

Arnold, N. W., Crawford, E. R., & Khalifa, M. (2016). Psychological heuristics and faculty of color: Racial battle fatigue and tenure/promotion. *The Journal of Higher Education, 87*(6), 890–919.

Boas, T., & Gans-Morse, J. (2009). Neoliberalism: From new liberal philosophy to anti-liberal slogan. *Studies in Comparative International Development, 44*(2), 137–161.

Berrett, D. (2016, November 5). The day the purpose of college changed. *The Chronicle of Higher Education*. Retrieved from www.chronicle.com/article/The-Day-the-Purpose-of-College/151359

Carruthers, C. A. [CharleneCac]. (2015, May 17). *When you're asked to talk about mass criminalization, occupation, hyper-militarization & it's not just for fun? It's tough emotional labor* [Tweet]. Retrieved from https://twitter.com/CharleneCac/status/599824463039827968

Carruthers, C. A. (2018). *Unapologetic: A black, queer, and feminist mandate for radical movements*. Boston, MA: Beacon Press.

Cohen, A. M., & Kisker, C. B. (2010). *The shaping of American higher education: Emergence and growth of the contemporary system*. San Francisco, CA: Jossey-Bass.

Cole, R. M., & Heinecke, W. F. (2018). Higher education after neoliberalism: Student activism as a guiding light. *Policy Futures in Education*. Retrieved from https://doi.org/10.1177/1478210318767459

DiAngelo, R. (2011). White fragility. *International Journal of Critical Pedagogy, 3*(3), 54–70.

Evans, L., & Moore, W. L. (2015). Impossible burdens: White institutions, emotional labor, and micro-resistance. *Social Problems, 62*, 439–454.

Ferguson, R. A. (2017). *We demand: The university and student protests*. Oakland, CA: University of California Press.

Freyd, J. J. (1996). *Betrayal trauma: The logic of forgetting childhood abuse*. Cambridge, MA: Harvard University Press.

Gaiter, A. (2018, March 27). Black emotional labor is core to my Columbia experience. *Columbia Spectator*. Retrieved from www.columbiaspectator.com/opinion/2018/03/28/black-emotional-labor-is-core-to-my-columbia-experience/

Gorski, P. C. (2019). Racial battle fatigue and activist burnout in racial justice activists of color at predominantly white colleges and universities. *Race Ethnicity and Education, 22*(1), 1–20.

Harrison, L. M. (2010). Consequences and strategies student affairs professionals engage in their advocacy roles. *Journal of Student Affairs Research and Practice, 47*(2), 197–214.

Harrison, L. M. (2014). How student affairs professionals learn to advocate: A phenomenological study. *Journal of College and Character, 15*(3), 165–178. doi:10.1515/jcc-2014-0020

Harrison, L. M., & Mather, P. C. (2017). Making meaning of student activism: Student activist and administrator perspectives. *Mid-Western Educational Researcher, 29*(2), 117–135.

Huerta, A. H., McDonough, P. M., & Allen, W. R. (2018). "You can go to college": Employing a developmental perspective to examine how young men of color construct a college-going identity. *The Urban Review, 50*(5), 713–734.

Johansson, A., & Vinthagen, S. (2016). Dimensions of everyday resistance: An analytical framework. *Critical Sociology (Sage Publications, Ltd.), 42*(3), 417–435.

Kenton, W. (2018). *Neoliberalism*. Retrieved from www.investopedia.com/terms/n/neoliberalism.asp.

Kezar, A. (2004). Obtaining integrity? Reviewing and examining the charter between higher education and society. *The Review of Higher Education, 27*(4), 429–459.

Kezar, A. (2010). Faculty and staff partnering with student activists: Unexplored terrains of interaction and development. *Journal of College Student Development, 51*(5), 451–480.

Linder, C., & Myers, J. S. (2017). Institutional betrayal as a motivator for campus sexual assault activism. *NASPA Journal about Women in Higher Education, 11*(1), 1–16. doi:10.1080/19407882.2017.1385489

Linder, C., Quaye, S. J., Stewart, T. J., Okello, W. K., & Roberts, R. E. (2017 November). *"The whole weight of the world on my shoulders": Power, identity, and student activism*. Paper presented at the annual meeting of the Association for the Study of Higher Education, Houston, TX.

Martin, G. L. (2014). Understanding and improving campus climates for activists. In C. J. Broadhurst, & G. L. Martin (Eds.), *"Radical academia"? Understanding the climates for campus activists* (Vol. 201, pp. 53–67). San Francisco, CA: Jossey-Bass. https://doi.org/10.1002/he

Martinez, E., & Garcia, A. (1997). *What is neoliberalism? A brief definition for activists*. Retrieved from https://corpwatch.org/article/what-neoliberalism

Northwest Ordinance, Article 3. (1787, July 13). (National Archives Microfilm Publication M332, roll 9); Miscellaneous Papers of the Continental Congress, 1774–1789; Records of the Continental and Confederation Congresses and the Constitutional Convention, 1774–1789, Record Group 360; National Archives.

Pierce, C. M. (1995). Stress analogs of racism and sexism: Terrorism, torture, and disaster. In C. Willie, P. Rieker, B. Kramer, & B. Brown (Eds.), *Mental health, racism and sexism* (pp. 277–293). Pittsburgh, PA: University of Pittsburgh Press.

Pippert, T. D., Essenburg, L. J., & Matchett, E. J. (2013). We've got minorities, yes we do: Visual representations of racial and ethnic diversity in college recruitment materials. *Journal of Marketing for Higher Education, 23*(2), 258–282. doi:10.1080/08841241.2013.867920

Quaye, S. J., Carter, K. D., Allen, C. R., Karikari, S. N., & Okello, W. K. (2018, November 17). *"Why can't I just chill?": The visceral nature of racial battle fatigue*. Paper presented at the annual meeting of the Association for the Study of Higher Education, Tampa, FL.

Quaye, S. J., Karikari, S. N., Allen, C. R., Okello, W. K., & Carter, K. D. (2018, November 15). *Strategies for practicing self-care from racial battle fatigue*. Paper presented at the annual meeting of the Association for the Study of Higher Education, Tampa, FL.

Rodgers, D. (2018). *The uses and abuses of "neoliberalism"*. Retrieved from www.dissentmagazine.org/article/uses-and-abuses-neoliberalism-debate

Rogers, I. (2012). *The black campus movement: Black students and the racial reconstitution of higher education, 1965–1972*. New York, NY: Palgrave Macmillan.

Saunders, D. (2007). The impact of neoliberalism on college students. *Journal of College and Character, 8*(5), 1–9.

Seal, A. (2018). How the university became neoliberal. *The Chronicle of Higher Education*. Retrieved from www.chronicle.com/article/How-the-University-Became/243622

Smith, C. P., & Freyd, J. J. (2013). Dangerous safe havens: Institutional betrayal exacerbates sexual trauma. *Journal of Traumatic Stress, 26*(1), 119–124.

Smith, C. P., & Freyd, J. J. (2014). Institutional betrayal. *American Psychologist, 69*(6), 575–587.

Smith, W. A., Allen, W. R., & Danley, L. L. (2007). "Assume the position . . . you fit the description": Psychosocial experiences and racial battle fatigue among African American male college students. *American Behavioral Scientist, 51*(4), 551–578.

Spade, D. (2017, February 10). Reframing faculty criticisms of student activism. *The Chronicle of Higher Education*. Retrieved from www.chronicle.com/article/Reframing-Faculty-Criticisms/239182

Stewart, T. J. (in press). "Where we are, resistance lives": Black women, social media, and everyday resistance in higher education. *The Journal Committed to Social Change on Race and Ethnicity, 5*(1).

Stewart, T. J., & Williams, B. (in press). Nuanced activism: A matrix of resistance. In A. Dache, S. J. Quaye, C. Linder, & K. McGuire (Eds.), *Rise up!: Activism as education*. East Lansing, MI: Michigan State University Press.

Sue, D. W. (2010). *Microaggressions in everyday life: Race, gender, and sexual orientation*. Hoboken, NJ: John Wiley & Sons, Inc.

Sui, O. M. (2015). *On the colonial legacy of U.S. universities and the transcendence of your resistance* [Keynote Transcript]. Retrieved from https://library.osu.edu/blogs/mujerestalk/2015/10/13/on-the-colonial-legacy-of-u-s-universities-and-the-transcendence-of-your-resistance/

Threads of Solidarity: WOC Against Racism. (2018, February 27). *How to compensate black women and femmes on social media for their emotional labor*. Retrieved from https://medium.com/@SolidarityWOC/pay-your-teachers-763d574c7d7f

Trudy. (2013, August 1). *Exploitation of black women's labor . . . In the name of feminism or justice? Please*. Retrieved from www.gradientlair.com/post/57089878980/black-women-labor-exploitation-by-mainstream-whites

PART II

Stories of Student Activists and Supportive Educators

Labor

Like the density of soaked clothing
Dripping as my feet anticipate each step
Noticing the puddle that trails behind me
Like a weighted vest to improve my strength
But never letting go of this vest
It follows me, pushes against me
Making me notice my presence in every space I occupy
Like moving through the world with dumbbells in my backpack
Resting alongside my books
Noticing their heaviness
As I calculate each step on campus
Seeing my peers lighter
Breathing more easily, not panting
Feeling free, effortless like consuming smogless air
Full of envy I observe them
But me, I labor, work
I toil carrying all the weight
On my body, my skin, my veins
Hoping for someone, anyone to take a pound or two
So that I can rest my weariness

Resistance

For some it's resistance
For some it's activism

For some it's existing
For some it's just showing up
Pushing against and between
Always fighting
Screaming to what often seems like an empty silence
Of apathy, of not noticing
Not remaining voiceless
Even when feeling isolated
Alone, like in an abandoned warehouse
Choosing
To agitate, nudge
Resisting the comfort of cozy privilege
Because what's the other option?

4

STUDENT ACTIVISTS' MOTIVATIONS, STRATEGIES, AND WISDOM

Mass media, scholars, and educators pay a great deal of attention to college student activists. Commentators and pundits label these students as armchair critics and snowflakes in broad brushstrokes, diminishing their labor and categorizing it as a form of foreclosing disagreement and discourse on college campuses. Media and campus figures critique student activists for not being grateful enough for the rights their forebears secured within the United States at best and playing identity politics or requiring codling at worst (e.g., Routledge, 2017; Svriuga, 2015). Rendering student activists across institutions as entitled propagandists paints student activists with too broad a brush. This harmful and lazy stereotyping of student activists remains particularly concerning for students with one or more minoritized identities. Ideologies of dominance, such as white supremacy, patriarchy, and heterosexism, allow for activists and their activism to be framed in this way. The students in our study tell a different story altogether. As active participants in the environments they seek to change, student activists engage in a complex critique of their campuses based on their daily experiences with power, oppression, and marginalization. Rather than being entitled or coddled, students' drive to change their campuses arises from their love for their institutions. This form of care prompts students to hold a mirror up to their institutions, demanding administrators deliver on the experiences and outcomes promised during recruitment through admission.

In this chapter, we discuss student activists' reflections on the wisdom they cultivated as a result of engaging in activism. First, we share the framing of wisdom versus learning or benefit that encapsulates what happened as a result of student activists' experiences. Second, we examine the motivations of students to engage their campuses and local communities via activism; many of the students' motivations are tied to their identities. Third, we discuss the strategies student activists leverage to engage their institutions, campus educators and administrators, and peers to inspire and, in some ways, push for change. Finally, we circle back to those aspects of wisdom activists cultivated as a result of engaging in activism.

Beyond Learning: The Wisdom of Engaging Activism

When discussing the relationship between activists and their activism, we wrestled with the word that typifies that nexus. While *learning* was salient for all of us, given our passions and backgrounds, it did not feel like enough, incorporating only one aspect of the relationship between activists and their activism. We worked to avoid positivist framings of activism as *affecting* students or participation in activism *resulting* in particular outcomes. Words like *benefit* evoked concepts of profit and rendered activism as something like a high-impact practice that should be replicated uncritically (e.g., Lange & Stewart, 2019). We challenge the benefit paradigm in Chapter 5 and elsewhere (Linder et al., 2019). Rather, we discuss the *wisdom* activists cultivated through their work as activists. Wisdom is not just about intelligence or experience. Wisdom requires the integration of experience, knowledge, and discernment. Wisdom includes generating further self-awareness, learning more about others, and developing as both students and citizens of the world. For us, activism was a means for students to *become wise*. Both the students in our study as well as those with whom we have worked in other settings have wrestled with their hopes for their communities while enduring the pain of marginalization. Through the strategies we discuss below, student activists practiced wisdom in how they engaged their campus environments, administrators, educators, and peers. Rather than being random, reactionary events, student activists' strategies for change combined their prior experiences, their own sources of knowledge, and mature levels of judgment.

Motivations for Engaging in Activism

The motivations that activists described in our study coalesced around four themes: identity, community, anger, and responding to local/national events. These four themes often overlapped with each other in students' narratives, as we note below. We made decisions about the placement of particular quotes dependent on the student's original motivation for getting involved in activism. For instance, if a student noted that they were primarily involved in activism because of their social identity but also saw their motivations as being based in a particular community, we placed them in the former theme. We discuss the four sets of motivations in the following sections reminding the reader of the permeability of these categories.

Identity-Based Motivations: Who I Am

Student activists wished to contribute to causes and communities that had a more direct tie to their social and personal identities. These motivations were more explicitly tied to students' articulation of their own social identities as a propellant to engage in activism. While there may be articulation of their work in the service of larger identity-based communities, the examples mentioned here refer to students who named their own identities as a motivation first and foremost. Student activists noted their desire to create identity-conscious or identity-specific spaces to support their communities. For Janet, a white, lesbian woman with an invisible disability, the desire to create such spaces was to combat the idea of "being the only (fill-in-the-blank)-identifying person on campus" around lesbian identity. Alongside a fellow lesbian-identifying peer, she worked to create more "women-specific programming." For Janet, the category of woman was expansive, not exclusive. Reflecting on her involvement in an LGBT student organization, she shared:

> The fact is, we didn't see any women who were participating. I thought that was a big problem because it's not like there are no lesbians out there, or bisexual women, or even trans women . . . I had a lot of pushback for that, which was really difficult, and was one of the reasons why, when I was a junior, I kind of ended up moving away from the LGBT community.

Janet worked to combat the cismale-centric nature of the LGBT student organization's leadership and membership. Despite the pushback, even after leaving the organization for a period of time, she continued to focus on women-specific initiatives because of her identity as a woman and "seeing the need to help women" whether they were straight, lesbian, queer, or trans.

For some, as we have discussed elsewhere in the book, their minoritized identity or identities made activism a given. When we asked Jason how his social identities influenced his work as an activist, he replied: "My knee-jerk response was I'm a Black man, what do you mean? What kind of question is that?" Continuing to answer the question after the interviewer further clarified, Jason shared:

> I've come to a point where I can see that my identity and I think my unapologetic presence can trigger a recovering racist to perhaps fall into default tendencies. The thing is that it really doesn't even have anything to do with me being a man because there are a lot of women who face perhaps increased struggles that I don't. Really just being a part of the Black community I think puts a lot of folks in the position to be obligated to do something. I was president of our Black Graduate Student Organization, and I had complaints from at least 10 people in my first year as president about faculty bullying and faculty racism that targeted especially black women.

Being a part of the Black community, Jason felt "obligated" to be a part of efforts to improve Black people's experiences in higher education.

Activists' social identities often went beyond broad racial organizing; it also went to the particularities. Alyssa, for instance, was involved in broader Asian

American student organizing on her campus but noted her particular experience of being "one of the very few" Cambodian Americans she knew on campus. She viewed her involvement in broader organizing being, in part, tied to her identity as a Cambodian American and being a member of her family, sharing:

> For me, it's been very important to be in that space because I get to remind other Asian Americans and folks outside of the Asian community that Cambodian Americans exist. I think that has been my main driver. Family and community is also a very important driver. I think even though I can't necessarily explain organizing or activist work to my family, I am doing it for them. They gave me opportunities here in the United States. It's the least I can do to try to make my community a better place.

While wanting to contribute to the broader Asian American community on her campus, Alyssa saw her activism intimately wrapped up with the representation of her identity as well as her family.

For others, family and home experiences provided a different kind of catalyst for action. These students experienced negative, and sometimes violent, home environments that motivated them to seek out tools for change. Growing up, Cora did not have positive role models within her home. She "grew up in a really dangerous and violent household," where her dad was "a dictator." By the time she left for college in the early 2000s, her negative experiences at home with her father inspired her "in a bad way" to help others who were situated in experiences that left them feeling powerless. She gained some role models during her undergraduate years, particularly the head of the women's studies program, who taught her about activism, how to go about intervening in violent situations, and how to get involved.

Zooming out from campus or family communities, some of the activists in our study found motivation in larger national conflicts between peoples. Ghassan came to the United States from Palestine; he noted that he continued to have family living under Israeli occupation in Palestine. He saw his "involvement, desire, and motivation" to be an activist and doing organizing work as indistinguishable from his identity or from where he was. Ghassan's identity and his racialized experiences in the United States fueled his activism. He shared:

> Being somebody who grew up in the [U.S.] South with my Arabic birth name meant that I was bullied and I got a lot of racism. That racist bullying politicized me. It made me ask a lot of questions. It made me ask questions regarding my religion. It made me ask questions regarding who I am. Through those questions, I discovered an entirely different world than I knew. This wasn't a good world, this was a pretty negative world. Through asking these questions, I stumbled upon not only the more grave detail of the Israeli colonial occupation, but I learned about U.S. imperialism.

> I learned about injustices in this country. I learned about the way many people have been struggling in the United States and around the world, against capitalism and economic policies that prioritize not them, but profit.

Not only did Ghassan's connection to the State of Palestine prompt his thinking around activism but also anti-Arab harassment he faced in schooling contexts. His identities, and others' reactions to his identities, prompted self-exploration that led him to explore injustice further.

Student activists also noted how others' reactions to and conceptions of their identities activated their involvement in advocacy and social change efforts. More specifically, activists discussed that prevailing stereotypes and dominant narratives of their identities and their communities compelled them to get involved on and off campus. When we asked Athena about the connection between her social identities and her work as an activist, she shared she was influenced because:

> I realized that people are talking about my identities who don't look like me and who don't have my identities as if they know about what's happening. I need to stand up and be an activist as a woman because it's not fair that men are making the decisions for me when they don't understand what it's like to be a woman. Now as an Asian woman, I also need to stand up and tell people this is what it's like to be in this situation, this identity, and so it has shaped a lot of what I currently am and I'm still struggling with it . . . like it needs to be part of a narrative because a lot of the things that's been written about, [they do not] focus on Asian women. I feel like we get stereotyped as being either too quiet and submissive or the dragon lady and stuff, like no we're not either of those and so a lot of what I do is very centered on like my identities and why I feel strongly about it.

Similar to others discussed so far, Athena felt she had little choice to be an activist. She did not want others, namely men, controlling the narrative about what it meant to be a woman generally or an Asian woman specifically.

Interestingly, those involved in identity-based activism did not only include minoritized students but also those with dominant identities. Eric, a self-described "white cismale from a middle-class family" noted his "duty" to work with and for minoritized communities on campus. He shared:

> A lot of people are scared to put their face out there for fear of being slandered or maybe being targeted by their peers, or maybe the community at large. I feel it's within my duty; I'm as white as you can get . . . People [for whom activism is risky] need to be able to look outside and know that there's someone speaking up for them, whether they be white, straight, or even someone who is completely different than me.

Eric's sense of duty to advocate for minoritized peoples did cross over into paternalistic attitudes. While noting how he worked alongside different groups of students, in particular, the LGBT community, he took a posture of "speaking for" rather than speaking with or alongside others. Eric's uncle passed away due to AIDS-related complications and made him feel he had "a moral obligation to speak for LGBT people, to make sure that all sorts of love" receives attention from different communities.

Somewhat similarly to Eric, Jamie, a white, bisexual woman, came to activism through both her minoritized and privileged identities. She noted how she "came from a pretty privileged background" as a "middle-class white girl in a fairly nice school district." Growing up, she tried to help her friends where she could but some resisted her paternalistic offers of help. With time, reflection, and a greater level of experience with gender- and sexuality-based oppression, Jamie thought more about her role in helping people within her own communities. She changed her course of study as a result of focusing on working with her own minoritized communities, "Why would I get an English degree when I instead could be doing something that will have a real impact on people?" While getting an English degree does not necessarily mean one cannot have an impact on others, Jamie's new double-major in public policy and social relations and women's studies gave her a clearer sense of connection to activism.

Community-Based Motivations: What I Care About

The student activists we interviewed largely indicated that being a part of particular communities motivated them to become activists or involved in advocacy work. Some activists developed community by becoming involved in activism. After a "rough transition" from high school to college, Marie, a white, cisgender, lesbian woman, noted an activist-oriented student organization in which she became involved that helped foster a sense of belonging to the institution. While she was sparingly involved in the organization during her first year in college, by her second year, she was a regular member. Propelled by "the people and the type of community [she] was brought into," the organization helped "inspire [her] own organizer journey," including learning more about concepts like privilege and intersectionality.

Many of the student activists discussed wanting to generate resources for marginalized communities, particularly since those resources did not appear to already exist on or off campus. During her first year in college, Rachel, a white, straight woman, was sexually assaulted. As a journalism major, she wrote an article about her experience and learned that there was not much institutional or interpersonal support for survivors. Many of Rachel's peers blamed women for making themselves vulnerable rather than putting an onus on the perpetrator of the assault. This lack of support prompted Rachel to reach out to her women's center director. She shared that the director

> introduced me to my now best friend; together, we just sat there and said, "What can we do?" We wrote the constitution in two hours, and then we spent the next week editing it, making sure it was appropriate for student government. She serves on student government, so she set up the meeting, and then we went and we just told them why it [having a dedicated student organization] was important in campus and needed approval, so we just kind of went from there.

Rachel and her co-organizer worked together to fulfill a need for a community they both thought had been rendered invisible on campus and needed greater levels of support.

Like Rachel, other students became part of communities that helped to contribute to their sense of belonging on and off campus. These students, in turn, became activists to reciprocate the work that had been done on their behalf. Lucia, a genderqueer white person, noted how gender-variant and polyamorous communities had helped them learn more about themselves and build platonic relationships with others. Their activism was "simply [their] way of giving back to those communities." Lucia's desire was not only to contribute to just their communities but also other communities.

Student activists connected their desires to contribute to communities and their academic pursuits. Rather than their academics being something disconnected from the campus and the local community, students often saw their activism being enhanced by their classroom-based learning. BLB, a biracial, cisgender woman, noted how "academic" and disconnected studying race in the workplace was before she got involved in the community. Working with different community groups, she shared:

> It feels like there's more of a practical need. It feels like I'm serving people that other people ignore. I feel like that community component has a lot to do with it, having access to communities that I didn't before, seeing what they define as issues, not necessarily what I read in a literature review. Things like that have had a big impact on me. Just exposure to the communities that I'm serving, that are not academic, that are not corporate managers.

While BLB had a desire to undertake research that would help racially minoritized people in the workplace, she did not want to wait to engage. Rather, she found she could work with employees currently while simultaneously completing her graduate coursework requirements.

Finally, motivated by the idea of creating something sustainable to follow their leadership, activists sought to generate change that would uplift those who came behind them. Jason believed activism was about "sacrificing" one's time and energy for something greater than oneself. Not only did this include thinking about what to address in the present but also how that carried to the future. Jason shared that leadership

> is never the onus of one individual. It reflects and engages the collective. When leadership creates [a] legacy, it's sustainable. It creates delegates that operate autonomously and engage in their own initiatives. In and of itself, I look at activism as the type of sacrifice that the self is removed and replaced with the collective to meet the collective needs and interest towards a progressive objective.

Jason noted the role of collectives not only in the present but also in the future. Not only were activists motivated by present-day members of their communities, but also the future members of those communities. Activism should not begin and end with certain leaders. This sentiment also carries over to those whose motivations were based on their social and personal identities.

Anger-Based Motivations: What I Am Reacting To

Like some of the student activists in both the community-based and identity-based motivations, some students' motivations for being activists were grounded in anger toward the object of their activism, which was often oppression. This anger was often rooted in students' frustrations that the institution's professed ideals or teachings (i.e., diversity, equity, inclusion, justice; Stewart, 2017) did not match its deeds and actions. We interviewed Lauren, a biracial, queer woman, after she had graduated from her institution. She noticed how the symbol for her college, human development and family studies, was a silhouette of a man, woman, and child. She felt angry that what she had learned within her studies in the college did not match what she was seeing in its symbolism, most notably a heterosexual, monogamous formation of a family. She started a petition to propose a change to the symbol since it "did not sit well" with her. She shared that she "did not like the way I petitioned. I did it out of anger instead of out of growth for the college." Rather than thinking "we can make this better together," she asked, "Why isn't this better already?" In reflection, Lauren wished her activism was grounded more in the former comment than the latter. The petition forced a vote for the college to change the symbol, propose a new symbol, and the vote passed.

Other activists took their anger and channeled it into their activism to facilitate education and change on campus. Danielle, a cisgender, straight, Black woman, noted the anger that many students, including her, felt at the failure of prosecutors to indict police officers for the death of an unarmed Black man in proximity to her institution. She shared how many students on campus were unsure of what should happen on campus to deal with the large amount "kinetic energy" on campus. "Kinetic energy" here meant the mix of deep anger and upset felt by many students on campus. Danielle and other activists focused this anger into a community-wide teach-in. She shared:

> Ten days after the failure [to indict the officer], we organized a community-wide teach in, so we could have conversations about what actually happened, where we need to go as a community, what we can do as a group to engage each other in a useful and a productive way. We just had an opportunity to let everything out. That was very significant and a very meaningful experience to be able to be a part of that and to be able to engage people in that manner, and that kind of social issue.

Danielle and other activists were able to direct their "kinetic energy" to the teach-in as a means to facilitate education and future social change on campus.

Danielle's experience with anger seemed to corroborate Lauren's theory about the nature and use of anger in student activism. Her theory held that while anger may be the impetus for activism, it is never how it ends. When asked what she learned from participating in activism she shared:

> Anger is good to start out with, in my opinion, but it's not sustainable. Especially for me, because I'm just doing my best. I've moved home recently and my parents have a very different political viewpoint than me, and coming at it with anger is not productive in their case and it just tires me out.

While allowing the room for anger to be a consistent motivator for others, Lauren made clear that it is not something that works in the long-term for her, whether that is long-term engagement with people who do not share her viewpoint or as a consistent motivator for her activism, as it just wears her out. Rather, as the next set of examples point out, students' motivations with anger are sometimes tied to particular events or contexts that allow for sustained engagement with emotional ties to activism.

Context-Based Motivations: Where I Am

In addition to community-based, identity-based, and anger-based motivations to engage in activism, students cited particular contextual influences and events that drove them to participate in social change efforts. For some, these motivations were local events that happened on campus. Pete, a South Asian genderqueer person, noted how repeated campus incidents that affected minoritized students got him more involved in campus-based activism. Violence committed against Students of Color activated Pete and other activists on their campus to advocate more for safe campus environments. Pete and others worked with administrators to create an advisory board to begin to address some of the issues. While Pete did not "necessarily think the advisory board is the way to create that kind of change," they nonetheless saw that as the university being "much more receptive to the things, the issues we've raised in protests."

Local- and state-level political forces and dynamics also motivated student activists to participate in advocacy efforts. Scarlet, a white, bisexual, cisgender woman, for instance, protested a bill in her state legislature that would have stripped away many resources for sexual violence survivors from college campuses. She described working with a small group of student activists to develop "a resistance" to the legislation, including developing social media and phone call campaigns and providing testimony during legislative committee hearings.

Zooming out further, widely publicized national events galvanized some students into forms of action. While we discuss the police shootings of unarmed Black men as a motivator for some students above, interpersonal violence against gay men like Matthew Shepard motivated students like Lee, a white, transgender, disabled graduate student, to become involved in campus activism. They shared:

> One of the very first things that impacted me as an activist was the death of Matthew Shepard. I was a sophomore in college at that time and it galvanized me as someone who was just exploring my own sexuality that could really happen to people just because they were gay or lesbian. I grew up in a sheltered Catholic environment. When I was young, I was just then exploring other sexualities other than heterosexuality and so it really hit me that people really hate. They really hate. It wasn't just the death that impacted me strongly, it was my campus's reaction to it. There was a candlelight vigil the night that he died on my campus. It was very cold; everybody was huddled together and in that moment, I realized the power of people.

Like other activists in our study, specific instances of violence enacted upon minoritized bodies motivated them to take action steps in their spheres of influence. While Lee was later involved in different forms of activism, the media display of Shepard's horrific beating helped push Lee into committing to do more with and for their community.

Students' motivations to undertake activism were vast and rarely one-dimensional. The motivations articulated by students connected to the categories we constructed above. While there was no single category of motivation from which activists pulled, it is critical to understand these motivations as they tie directly to the enacted strategies for change.

Strategies to Enact Change

As we write this book, students across the United States continue to organize, often with others, to enact change on their college campuses. Their strategies are multifaceted. As the activists in our study demonstrated, there are many ways to be an activist and engage in activism. As Marie shared, student activists "start with what [they] have." Some student activists engage in organizing efforts that are often more readily recognized as activism. This includes organizing rallies and events and vigils on campus and in local communities. Other strategies include having an online presence; being present in online activism is critical given the investment young adults have in social medias (Subrahmanyam, Reich, Waechter, & Espinoza, 2008; van Dijck, 2013). This online presence allows for different articulations of why particular issues merit more attention.

For Marie, activism meant taking a step beyond allyship, sharing that "I've always viewed activism as a step further. I've always thought being an ally is a verb, it's not an identity. And being an activist, being involved, financially giving to organizations that need it, showing up to planning meetings" is a way to take this next step. Indeed, both the activists we have worked with as educators, as well as the students in our study, demonstrated that their activism is a verb: these students enact several strategies to facilitate conversation and change on their campuses and in their local communities. We discuss five broad areas of strategy that student activists in our study engaged: educating for change, working within and outside of formal systems, working in solidarity with other communities and issues, practicing self-care, and fostering more activists.

Educating for Change

While the more direct-action forms of activism, like marches and sign-wielding protests, receive a great deal of attention, much of the long work of activism is that of disseminating and spreading knowledge about communities and issues. In many ways, the direct-action style of activism is meant to raise awareness about an issue; once activists have raised awareness, capitalizing on the awareness is imperative. For instance, when doing work to curb sexual violence on campus through her new student organization, Rachel "realized that people needed more education." She shared:

> [We brought] articles into our club and discussed them. Something like the Brock Turner Stanford trial, following that, and talking about how much rape culture affects our communities and our campuses. [We also taught members] important vocabulary that they would need to know, like "what is rape culture," because I think for somebody who's already read the literature, it's easy to just steamroll through these conversations.

Rachel recognized how fundamental concepts and language were necessary to help people understand rape culture and recognize it in their daily experiences. Some activists can just "steamroll" through the conversations because of their deep knowledge of these issues; however, although not everyone shares this deep knowledge, they may still be compelled to help address the issue in question.

For some activists, spreading knowledge looked like the format Rachel's group adopted. Some student activists, because of the lack of organizational support at their institutions, developed training sessions or panels for faculty, staff, and students. For instance, Zi, an Asian genderqueer person, shared how their group does an annual LGBTQ 101 panel during the early part of the school year:

> We try and do [the panel within the first] 2–3 weeks, a month after people have moved in, in case you might have a roommate who is queer, you might have somebody in your class that you're working with or something like that . . . this is primarily directed at educating allies and changing the culture [at the institution]. One of the hardest things about activism and awareness is that you're trying to change people's minds, and it's really easy to preach to the choir. One of the major problems that a lot of these groups run into is you get the same people coming back to all of your events, which is fantastic that they care, but you need new people to also talk to.

Zi spoke to the same dynamic Rachel alluded to: if one is to educate allies and change the culture of a community or an institution, one must reach "new people" and engage them in both conversation and education. Zi's group decided to take up some of the labor of doing gender and sexuality education on campus rather than leave it to other LGBTQ students.

For other activists, rather than engaging in co-curricular education initiatives, they preferred to generate and facilitate dialogue between different people. These activists focused their efforts on process rather than outcome and wrestled with what that meant. For instance, when we asked Eric, a straight, white, cisgender man, why he got involved in activism, he noted that he wanted to start a dialogue. When asked to elaborate, he shared:

> It's been interesting, trying to find the right dialogue, because as you know, after the [2016] U.S. presidential election, people are inquiring whether the best route is to do solidarity, to take up a non-aggressive stance. [For me,] a dialogue would be a mutual understanding and mutual care for one another. Mostly giving people the tools to succeed without alienating people. That's been one of the main things that I have struggled with. What is the right conversation to have? What is the right message? How do you go about it?

Eric wrestled with the tension between combative and "non-aggressive" forms of activism and dialogue. He wanted a way to bring people together to work on making a better world but was unsure if this was the right course if there was such a thing.

Other activists used classroom and event-based spaces to spread knowledge about the communities they advocated on behalf of; the engagement in these spaces depended on the audience's disciplinary intentions. For instance, Lucia discussed how they engage those who are in human service disciplines, such as social work, education, or counseling psychology. Rather than overwhelm them with facts and figures, Lucia helps them puzzle through the question of "why is it moral or immoral to look at someone in a certain light?" Lucia tied education directly to social change, hoping that "later on down the line, that does lead to policy change" and that until they had the power to change policy themselves, education was "the best" Lucia could do.

The graduate students in our study, particularly those who formally taught courses at their institutions, used their teaching to spread knowledge about certain communities. For Athena, a Filipino, straight, cisgender woman, it was critical to disrupt the Black-white binary that permeates much of the race discourse in the United States. Discussing her facilitation of a class on the prominence of representation of Black and white people in the United States, she shared:

> [Discussing representation of a broad array of People of Color] matters to us because it makes it seem like other People of Color are just allies and that they don't have their own struggles. And so I push the narrative being discussed in class, telling people, "Have you thought about other People of Color and their struggles? Do you know about our history?"

Later, Athena discussed how she began to trouble the idea that domestic discourses of multiculturalism were separated from the ways international students are racialized when they come to the United States. These discourses justified separating these students into what Athena believed were artificial categories that prevented coalition-building.

Averi, a white, agender, queer person, also taught courses at the undergraduate level and discussed her strategies to be intentional with her syllabus to expose students to ideas they may not have questioned before. For instance, she gave the example of a human sexuality course she taught at her institution. She described walking students through "what historically led [people] to think of sexuality" and "what led research to be what it is" while "not trying to condemn anyone but [shedding] light onto what we consider normative and what we consider identifiable." This form of teaching the course "allowed people to find where they are on a spectrum [of knowledge] rather than just learning very heteronormative, usually Christian-based, ideas." For Averi, teaching was her engagement in activism.

Others developed opportunities and spaces for others to engage and learn. Jason worked to develop a conference for high school students to learn about and discuss "social justice around issues that concern them." While some developed spaces, others worked on projects to spread knowledge and awareness. Janet worked on a history project about LGBTQ activism to help those who were not exposed to such information early on. Noting the uniqueness of how LGBTQ people are often not raised by LGBTQ parents, she shared:

> What I've been working on is a project to remember past activists. I think that's a really huge problem because a lot of young kids don't even know

> [about the AIDS epidemic]; I think it's almost unforgivable that we haven't been [taught it in K–12 schools] . . . When you are LGBT, it's not like you grew up with LGBT parents necessarily. You don't have anyone to teach you the history. You don't get gay history in high school. Unless people are looking for [this information], they don't necessarily find anything. Sometimes they don't even know what to be looking for. I know when I was 17, 18, I had no idea what to be looking for.

Janet shared her work to cultivate information for young people to know who and what came before them. Educating others became her work in activating others and larger numbers of people becoming interested in social change.

Finally, some activists used education efforts to facilitate and advocate for policy change on campus. Scarlet worked to edit the sexual misconduct policy of her institution. She began by creating a Facebook page to garner awareness of what she viewed as necessary changes to the policy while building initial support. This experience led her to work with an organization that wrote reports to share information about improvements to policies. The group not only worked to research policy alternatives, but advocated for them as well. Members of Scarlet's group "worked at the [state] capital a lot," while she went "more the student government route." Working with a coalition of students across several state institutions, Scarlet and others in the group worked to have their student governments declare particular positions on state bills while activating grassroots measures like letter-writing campaigns. While the initial work was around education, as seen with others below, student activists worked within and outside of formal structures to facilitate change on campus.

Working Within and Outside Formal Systems

The student activists in our study recognized both the power and limitations of formal systems (e.g., student government, state government) to facilitate social change on and off campus. With this recognition came different strategies to work within, around, and outside of these systems to push for the change they wished in their work. For instance, Alyssa served as a formal leader within her student government, which gave her "access to speaking with upper administrators, including vice presidents, vice chancellors, vice provosts, and chancellor." Alyssa admitted she would not have had such access to these people without this role. She noted the importance of creating relationships with these people "to bring legitimacy to the work" she was trying to do on campus in terms of community organizing. As time passed, however, Alyssa became a graduate student and did not establish relationships with new administrators. Administrators questioned Alyssa's organizing of alumni against the institution in some way. She described this as "very interesting" and continued to believe it was important to organize for change both within systems but later outside them as well.

Alyssa was not the only activist who went to administrators' spaces to voice concerns. Unlike Alyssa, however, administrators perceived other activists to be more confrontational in their methods to facilitate change on campus. Marie shared:

> Right now, we are in the process of showing up to higher administration meetings. Usually, from the path of business [and agenda items], this hasn't been super effective, but that's always the first step. [We've attended] faculty summits and board of trustee meetings. We have [social media campaigns] running with hashtags and spreading our message that way. There hasn't been any talk of rallies yet but I wouldn't be surprised if it got that far.

For Marie and other activists, confronting administrators through demonstrations was only one step in a broader plan to achieve change on campus. Later, she noted how administrators (i.e., the university president, provost, and vice president of student affairs) were about to conduct a listening tour on campus to hear about different organizations' concerns about the institution. Student activists, including Marie, were skeptical of the aims of the administrators and thought further about engaging them differently under this format.

Like other activists, some students developed their own organizations within university parameters to access the benefits of being associated with either their student government or institution. As we began to discuss above, Rachel and her friend developed their own organization, which included authoring a constitution, hosting their first meeting, electing officers, and presenting all this information to their student government to get formal organizational approval. Developing this organization continued to be a formal lever of promoting change on campus. After getting approval from student government, Rachel and other organization officers met with the student government marketing team to "promote themselves and their message on campus" and encouraged their elected student leaders to allow one of their members "to serve on a task force that was working to better address the needs of students" as it related to sexual violence. While not being elected to student government themselves, Rachel and others used the student organization registration process as well as the resources provided to official organizations to further spread awareness and work toward change around sexual violence on campus.

Some of the activists in our study noted how their thinking shifted across their time at the institution. For instance, Pete shared that they "used to think that working with an institution would always be beneficial" and "that people would respect [them] depending on how [they] framed arguments." However, when Pete was not met with that respect, regardless of how they discussed their points of view, they shared,

> I realized it was more [important] for me to choose not to silence myself because I understood that I would be institutionally silenced no matter

> how I said something; I understood I [needed to believe in myself] and that being more respectable [would not change the way people viewed me] . . . I think that created a large shift in the way that I view things [related to activism].

For Pete, this shift and being silenced became a commitment to direct action against the institution. For instance, after the 2016 U.S. Presidential election, Pete and other activists worked to make Pete's campus a sanctuary campus. At first, the institution's administrators had a stance that it would share immigration and documentation status with anyone from the federal government who requested such information. After the election, however, students "organized a walkout" during class sessions, promoting the institution to reverse course and only provide information pursuant to federal laws. Pete and other activists demonstrated that outside pressure via direct action against the institution can help achieve particular results that working within an institution would never prompt.

Working in Solidarity

The activists in our study, as well as those in our personal experiences, often worked across communities and issues; these activists cultivated an ethic of solidarity with other activists to build community and think through issues with multiple communities in mind. Jamie, a student leader who was part of a group that brought together different LGBTQ student organizations on campus, discussed the importance of developing community across different student organizations. She shared:

> All of the [organizations] are queer-centric, and the leaders meet every other week to just discuss what's going on and build community. It's pretty unprecedented, actually. Before this, the [organizations] were totally separate, they didn't really interact very much. Certain [organizations] were more or less on their own. I think one of my bigger accomplishments is really getting this [umbrella group] to where I want it to be as a community builder. Especially, [U.S. presidential] post-election. This time is going to be a trying one for us in the [LGBTQ] community more than ever. It's going to be really important [to work together]. We'll need to pool resources and pool knowledge.

Jamie named several reasons for the student organizations on her campus to work together. In addition to not being isolated from each other, the organizations could work together to look out for each other, sharing their resources and capabilities in service to the larger LGBTQ+ campus community.

Activists understood solidarity and connection between different groups and movements as critical to their own work. Lee shared the importance and "power of people raising their voices together." While certain movements may be more visible outside one's geographic region (e.g., Occupy Wall Street, Black Lives Matter), Lee "felt connected to [these movements] because we stand for the same things and we are moving toward the same goals. That connection to people everywhere that have the same intent" is "very powerful" and "keeps me motivated." While not necessarily being in physical proximity to each other, Lee noted how the mere existence and witnessing of other social change movements continued to galvanize their own work in their own region of the United States.

Solidarity work was not always a physical enactment; for some, their activism helped them to think more about and foreground communities with multiple, marginalized identities. When we asked Jamie what she had learned from being an activist, she noted how intersectional identities became more foregrounded in her psyche and meaning-making. Noting that in high school she focused more on her own marginalized identities (i.e., her identities of being bisexual, Jewish, and woman-identifying), her activist work in college helped shift her thinking about the struggles of multiple communities, particularly racially minoritized communities among other groups of people. Through a combination of her coursework and involvement, she learned that systems of oppression are "so interconnected and overlapping that in order to dismantle any of them [one needs] to be focusing on everyone." This focus on everyone contrasted with just looking at the communities of which she shared a marginalized positionality.

For some, this work in solidarity with others prompted them to think about their frameworks for making sense of activism. While many students in our study and in our experiences generally thought of their activism through their particular issue, or identity-based lens, some students, like Pete, thought about their activism using different frameworks given particular issues. Pete shared:

> Our entire framework is that we organize around any issue . . . or inequalities on campus while also understanding and tackling the anti-Black framework the United States [and the whole world] operates under. So, if we're talking about sexual violence, we prioritize understanding sexual violence against trans Women of Color . . . because we think that organizing around the margin is really important because when you organize around the margin, you organize for everybody.

Going one step further than Jamie, Pete articulated a particular framework that they use for all of their activism. While Jamie noted how an intersectional approach to activism is necessary to dismantle interconnected and overlapping systems of oppression, Pete's articulation of a framework that focused on those on the margins of society is similar to a framework articulated by Spade (2015). In short, by centering a group most on the margin (e.g., transgender Women of Color), addressing the inequalities this group faces would also address the inequalities of those along various gender and racial positionalities. This framework of activism was key to Pete's engagement with campus issues, which demonstrates a complex form of meaning-making as we discuss elsewhere (Quaye & Lange, 2018).

Practicing Self-Care

Student activists understood how their labor to change their institutions affected them personally. While they were dedicated to spreading knowledge, working within and outside of formal systems, and thinking through and enacting solidarity across groups, student activists knew they needed to take care of themselves and attend to their needs in order to make their activism sustainable. These forms of self-care varied. For instance, Danielle leaned on prayer as a form of taking care of herself. She set up particular boundaries for herself to reclaim her energy after long weeks, specifically making a rule that she did nothing on Sundays. She shared how Sundays were her day, when she "reads, watches movies, eats, goes to church, and that's it." Danielle "decided a long time ago that there's a good reason why there's one day of the week that [one] should just not work, just rest, and take care of [oneself]." Danielle was unapologetic about her taking Sundays for herself—she needed this day to tackle the rest of the week's work.

Rather than having a regimented day where one took a break, others' boundaries were established more as they became necessary. For instance, Athena noted that she would "take a step back from all of it" at times. This step back included removing herself from social media, going to talk to her support systems, and processing what was happening in her life at the moment. She further shared:

> Sometimes I really do need to just walk away from it, go away for a weekend or something if I can, or just stay in my room and sleep just to recharge myself and take care of myself. Sometimes I have to take . . . a mental health day where I cancel all my appointments . . . I need to take care of myself before I can take care of my students.

Athena noted how she took time for herself when she felt she was at her limit. While she did not appear to have a regular practice to help her avoid burnout continuously, Athena knew when she was approaching her limits and acted accordingly.

Other activists, like Jamie, needed to practice discernment in deciding when to be on campus. For instance, Jamie's commitment to multiple student organizations prompted her to think about when a meeting was essential to something on which she had been working. While Jamie acknowledged that "every meeting feels essential," academic due dates required her to make decisions about when and where to show up. This level of discernment helped Jamie know when meetings or particular engagements were more necessary versus knowing she could focus more on writing papers for class.

At times, activists had to make decisions to remove themselves from an activist space. In Janet's case, this removal was about the activist space itself becoming toxic and needing to direct her energy elsewhere. When members of the on-campus LGBTQ student organization resisted her focus on woman-centric programming, Janet found herself walking away from the organization for which she devoted such a great deal of time. Rather than continue to focus on that organization, she directed her energy elsewhere, stating:

> I literally just went to the domestic violence shelter, and I spent time with [the staff and the women staying there]. I spent a lot more time work. I picked up tons of hours . . . I literally did not have any contact [with the LGBTQ student organization], and I felt like an outcast. It was really, really tough. It took me that year to grow, to see, "Okay, no I'm not really doing the wrong thing. No, I'm not the devil incarnate for daring to be a lesbian who spoke and tried to make women-centric programming." Now I've been able to come back around and contribute to the community again.

Rather than stopping her activism altogether, Janet redirected her energy elsewhere because of her desire to continue giving herself to a particular cause.

Fostering More Activists

Student activists, most likely due to their awareness that their status as students was always temporary, focused on developing and cultivating a new generation of activists to follow behind them. For some activists like Rachel, this meant working with others and developing the awareness that the work of activism was not just about one person's ideas. Specifically, Rachel stated that she realized "not every idea had to be [her] idea" and that being a good leader meant "stepping back and letting other people grow a really great idea" that would profoundly affect campus.

Janet and Jamie found it critical to develop the next generation of activists who would follow their work and labor on campus. As Jamie was considering her legacy on campus, she discussed how she inadvertently was "grooming the next generation" as she worked on campus. While she "may be gone one day," she knew the "concepts [she] taught somebody will still be around" after that. While Jamie's cultivation of future activists was somewhat unexpected, Janet's could be described as more intentional. She shared:

> I don't want to be doing all the work. If I can give some other students, "You do this part, you do this part, and then next year I'm not going to be here but I want you to keep working on this part" . . . I think that's the way we foster a community of activists who are really engaged in what they're doing, who know that there are people there to support them, even if other people say, "You're doing the wrong thing," and then who will continue to do this, and then foster other activists.

For Janet, nurturing the next generation of activists required splitting up the work and labor of particular activist projects while developing a support system for those new activists to rely upon while they learned the ways to be activists.

The cultivation and generation of new student activists also came from understanding that change was a generational effort. Lee understood any "attempt at progress [being] generational." While they once acknowledged change as something to expect immediately from institutions, Lee learned that viewing change in this way would leave one "really disappointed" and eventually lead to burnout and disenchantment. Over time, Lee came to appreciate that change is a "very slow process" and that real change "takes time, even centuries" to achieve.

Students' strategies to enact change on their campus were varied and depended on their experiences, personal dispositions, and what was happening on their campuses. While many readers (and activists) may expect more strategies than these five categories, we lift these up intentionally as tactics one might not expect from student activists on college campuses. These strategies are as much about *doing* something as they are about *being* something. Activists' strategies were multifaceted and engaged not only their cognitive skills but also their relational knowing and physical engagement. These three facets of activists' strategies bring us back to the ways they cultivated wisdom through their activism.

Cultivating Wisdom

> I think [being white] influences my activism a lot. When I was younger or newer to activism, I would always tell myself that in order to have a focus [on a particular issue], you cannot be good at everything. I cannot know every issue . . . the only thing I can do is listen and try. Over the years, I've learned that really isn't enough. That was a cop out so I didn't have to learn and attend to the issues that I don't have to deal with for being white. And so, I've tried to shift my activism. [Rather than giving into white guilt], I am recognizing whenever I say something that I'm using as an excuse [to avoid further learning] . . . [I've learned] to give myself space without forgiving myself for it entirely. I'll be like, "It's okay that you don't know this now, but it's important that you try. You can't just decide what you care about is enough activism" . . . As an activist, I've realized the limitations of my activism, and of my personal understanding of documentation status and race.
>
> —*Averi*

Through both their motivations to engage in activism as well as their strategies to achieve their aims, student activists learned more about themselves, the issues for which they advocated, and the world around them. As Averi noted, she learned more and more about what and who she was missing while she advocated for certain issues and communities. Rather than passive learning, however, this awareness came with new ways of knowing, being, and doing in regard to her activism; she was not alone. Engaging in activism engendered more than new knowledge in these activists—activists cultivated a particular kind of wisdom they carried with them during the remainder of their institutional experience and beyond.

Wisdom ranged from the technical to the complex. Janet learned about the logistics of running a domestic violence shelter and gained a certain level of discernment about what she can and cannot do in regard to social service professions in the future. Scarlet gained insight into the ways to mobilize others and center the experiences of those with minoritized identities. Jason became wiser by understanding what it meant to share the microphone and bullhorn with others, particularly those with different levels of formalized education compared to him. He came to understand that having college degrees did not make him any better than those who did not.

Student activists embodied the lessons they carried with them from engaging in activism. Pete carried the complexity of marginalization with them. As a self-identified "non-Black Person of Color," Pete understood how they experienced racism but not anti-Blackness and how they held both marginalized and privileged identities. This deeper understanding affected the way Pete organized social change efforts and the issues with which they engaged. Lucia understood how certain issues and activism were "in vogue" or "fashionable." They discussed the whiteness behind activism for LGBTQ communities, particularly by middle-class white cisgender men and women. In Lucia's view, these groups of people relegated issues that required greater levels of intersectional thought to the margins of conversations. McKenzie's eyes opened to the possibility that people could begin to comprehend her oppression even if they did not share identities or life experiences with her. Working in solidarity with others helped McKenzie understand that movements need broad-based coalitions to sustain themselves and push for greater levels of change.

As we discuss in the next chapter, while activists cultivated a certain level of wisdom as a result of participating and engaging in activism, we do not wish to impart activism as something that has only benefits for students. Rather, as the students in our study, as well as those with whom we have worked in our previous roles, have demonstrated, involving oneself in activism becomes a form of unpaid labor that drains activists' energy and resources.

References

Lange, A. C., & Stewart, D. L. (2019). High-impact practices. In E. S. Abes, S. R. Jones, & D. L. Stewart (Eds.), *Rethinking college student development theory using critical frameworks*. Sterling, VA: Stylus.

Linder, C., Quaye, S. J., Lange, A. C., Roberts, R. E., Lacy, M. C., & Okello, W. K. (2019). "A student should have the privilege of just being a student": Student activism as labor. *The Review of Higher Education, 42*, 37–62.

Quaye, S. J., & Lange, A. C. (2018, November). *Pete's letter: A student activist's message to campus administrators*. Paper presented at the annual meeting of the Association of the Study of Higher Education, Tampa, FL.

Routledge, C. (2017, December 19). The academic left holds us all back by playing identity politics. *National Review*. Retrieved from www.nationalreview.com/2017/12/academic-left-radical-identity-politics-threaten-american-progress/

Spade, D. (2015). *Normal life: Administrative violence, critical trans politics, and the limits of law* (2nd ed.). Durham, NC: Duke University Press.

Stewart, D. L. (2017, March 30). Language of appeasement. *Inside Higher Ed*. Retrieved from www.insidehighered.com/views/2017/03/30/colleges-need-language-shift-not-one-you-think-essay

Subrahmanyam, K., Reich, S. M., Waechter, N., & Espinoza, G. (2008). Online and offline social networks: Use of social networking sites by emerging adults. *Journal of Applied Developmental Psychology*, *29*, 420–433. doi:10.1016/j.appdev.2008.07.003

Svriuga, S. (2015, November 30). College president: 'This is not a day care. This is a university!'. *The Washington Post*. Retrieved from www.washingtonpost.com/news/grade-point/wp/2015/11/30/college-president-rejects-safe-spaces-writing-this-is-not-a-day-care-this-is-a-university/?noredirect=on&utm_term=.49842b837448

van Dijck, J. (2013). "You have one identity": Performing the self on Facebook and LinkedIn. *Media Culture Society*, *35*(2), 199–215.

5

STUDENT ACTIVISM AS LABOR

> I had two different meetings with different administrators; I was called to represent all gays, basically. An administrator [also] came to speak to our executive board, to see what our concerns are. Nothing really changed. We still don't have gender-neutral bathrooms, and that was our number one thing that's really easy change to just do . . . It's a $12 sign to change any single stall.
>
> —*Janet, white, lesbian, cisgender woman with an invisible disability*

Because of Janet's identities, administrators often call on her to offer solutions to address LGBT campus issues, in this case gender-neutral bathrooms. As a result of administrators' requests, Janet had to determine if she had the time to engage with administrators about the issue, and if administrators would actually implement her recommendations. In addition to her personal meeting, Janet also had to create time to hear from the administrator during an executive board meeting, frustrated about the performativity of the gesture. Janet spent considerable time on meetings and emails and organizing with administrators to engage about the issues, which interfered with her opportunity to just be a student and focus on her academic pursuits (Linder et al., in press). As such, her words illustrate an example of labor that student activists with minoritized identities perform, and in Janet's case specifically, she still did not receive the $12 sign.

Postsecondary institutions continue to be spaces where people with dominant identities and in positions of power oppress students with minoritized identities, leading to trauma (Linder et al., in press). As a result, students with minoritized identities often engage in activism as a way to hold their institutions accountable for addressing oppression. Their activism is a form of labor they feel compelled to perform and something in which students with dominant identities do not have to engage. What we mean by labor is that students are engaged in work—writing demands to administrators, protesting, meeting with administrators, and organizing with their peers—beyond the bounds of what they expected they would be doing as college students.

In addition to their physical labor, the labor of identity-based student activists also has mental and emotional costs attached to them, including exhaustion, lack of sleep, and anxiety, which contribute to poor health. These physical, mental, and emotional consequences taken together with their student realities engender incredibly difficult experiences for them on their respective campuses as they work to create change and make them better.

In this chapter, we discuss student activism as student labor. Student activists' labor has emotional, mental, and physical costs, as well as specific institutional benefits. We begin with sharing findings from our study to underscore the particular ways activists engaged in labor and the costs of their activism. We close this chapter with discussing key takeaways, including the specific benefits institutions receive from activists' labor.

Participants' Stories of Labor: Costs and Consequences

Participants' stories illuminate the challenges and labor associated with activism, which affected them in the following three ways: isolation, emotional trauma, and schoolwork suffering. Before discussing these three elements, we discuss the notion of unpaid labor to give readers context for the damaging ways students' labor negatively impacted them but benefited the institution.

Unpaid Labor

Perhaps the most insidious consequence of students engaged in activism was the way institutions benefited from their labor. Students arrived on their campuses to be college students, not expecting to be activists. Yet, they needed to engage in activism as a way to survive in their minoritized bodies and address oppression on their campuses. Averi, a white, queer, agender person, summarized this:

> When I present to people, they just see a nice person who really, really cares and wants to help. When they see that person, they don't first think, "Let me pay them for their services." Then, I'm stuck. They'll ask me to do something. Then, I'll be like, "Yeah, that sounds like something I want to do. Absolutely." Then, if I ask later how much I'm going to get paid, they'll be like, "Well, why do you need to get paid?" The choice is I do it for free, or I don't do it. It's hard for me to choose don't do it. That doesn't feel good. It won't feel good emotionally. I just get put in a lot of really icky situations.

The "really icky situations," as conveyed by Averi, are the tensions in doing activism for free or asking for compensation. Given her care for improving her institution, she often chose to engage without compensation. However, that choice did not "feel good emotionally."

Based on the experiences and stories offered by participants, it seems relatively easy for administrators and educators to render invisible the ways students generally provide labor to their campus communities. Educators often fail to see how they contribute to labor demands on students, even when they have good intentions. For example, in asking activists to participate in the study, we did not compensate them for their time and also took time away from other activities in which they could be engaged. Averi also spoke to this point:

> I think activists have this addiction to caring and forgetting that they also matter. Because of that, they can run into a lot of problems. I participated in tons of research studies on activism. I loved doing that. I care about that. But like I said before, after doing this interview with you, how much am I going to continue doing activism? This hour could've been spent instead doing something to emotionally just help myself rather than helping the community. How many hours a day do I spend caring about the community and the greater issues more so than myself? In the long run, how many people will that end up hurting? The activists who just get drained.

Averi noted a real problem among activists—caring so much for others that they often did not prioritize their own needs. In some ways, people in positions of power exploit this care among activists without proper compensation, or even a recognition that the students are engaging in a form of labor and service to the work of their institutions.

A white, straight, able-bodied woman, Rachel, discussed the financial implications of her activism. She mentioned how the student organization of which she was a part, as well as her advisor, demanded much time from her, and yet she needed a job to be able to pay her bills:

> Our advisor [was] questioning how much I was working at the gym. Looking back, I made a commitment to the organization by being president, and I should have made sure I was there to be approachable to people, and so I think that taught me a lot about accountability that way, and if you say you're going to do it, you have to continue, and about being transparent about your actions with other people. So, letting them all know, "I love you guys, but I'm really scared that I'm not going to have money to live off of when I have to accept an unpaid internship this summer."

Needing to prioritize her finances was tricky for Rachel; she feared not being able to live given the very real implications of her activism. Not only was Rachel in a volunteer role within her organization, she also had to prepare for an unpaid summer internship opportunity. Her story illustrates the complex nature of identity-based student activists as it relates to trying to *survive* in the world and wanting to *thrive* on their campuses.

Teresa, a Latina cisgender woman from a low-income background, effectively summarized the free labor in which activists engaged. When asked what she wants administrators to know about her activism, she responded:

> Acknowledging the fact that if they're asking for meetings, they're taking time away from students' academics. There should be some sort of compensation for that, even if it is buying them lunch or buying them dinner. You're alleviating some of the other things that the student has to worry about. It should not just always be taking from the student, and I don't think they acknowledge that that's what they're doing a lot of the time. They just think, "Oh, this is a good student." There should be compensation for all of these conversations and meetings and working groups in some form. A student should have the privilege of just being a student, and it's just really weird how that is a privilege, just being a student, but it obviously is because there are people who cannot only be students.

Given Teresa's minoritized identities, engaging in activism without compensation was challenging. Because some students appear to be doing well academically, administrators asked for their time to help them understand how to improve their campuses to better meet activists' needs. As Teresa explained, lack of compensation for their time and labor creates a burden for activists and something as simple a meal would have helped fill a material need for activists working to improve their campus communities. Teresa also effectively illustrated that there are people who cannot only be students, something she identifies as a privilege. It is troublesome that "just being a student" is a privilege to which only some students have access. All students should have the right to just being a student, a reality that currently eludes identity-based student activists in multiple ways.

Isolation

Student activists described often feeling isolated in their activism. Working to hold administrators accountable for addressing oppression resulted in not having many allies or supporters and feeling alone. Alyssa, an Asian American, heterosexual, cisgender woman, said, "Being an activist also comes with stereotypical perceptions of what an activist is." Some of these stereotypes include "being intimidating or 'She's too serious. She's not fun. We can't invite her to things because she's just going to talk about privilege and oppression.' There's a perception of an activist that may not sit well with people." Peers' assumptions about activists led participants to feel misunderstood, which contributed to them feeling isolated.

A biracial, heterosexual, cisgender woman, BLB, discussed burning bridges and the isolation that caused:

> My old advisor and I do not talk. I won't really even look at her if we're in the same room. There's other bridges I probably burned that I'm not even aware of with other faculty and students. In burning bridges, I mean they don't necessarily want to work with me or they're not going to go out of their way to help me. I wouldn't ask them for letters of recommendation even though I worked with one of them for three years and did a lot of stuff for her.

Working closely with her advisor, BLB expressed how this relationship suffered as a result of her activism. BLB is a graduate student, so burning bridges meant losing support and potential future opportunities, given the power advisors have in students' future through letters of recommendation, referrals, and other gatekeeping practices in higher education.

Some participants indicated that they experience loneliness as a result of their identity as activists with minoritized identities, specifically. For example, Athena, a Filipino woman who also noted that she is limited in her mobility, commented: "It can be very lonely being an activist, especially when you have marginalized identities because it's hard to find that support system or other people who will understand what you're going through." Athena's words highlight the differences in her experiences and specifically what she perceives are the differences between activists like herself and those with more dominant social identities.

Participants also shared feelings of loneliness and isolation through experiences that are unique to them, those that they believe are connected to their specific activist issues and causes. For example, Ghassan shared a story about feeling constantly watched and monitored:

> We would be sitting and tabling at [building], and somebody would come and take a picture of us and just walk away. When they take that picture, we're already thinking about how this can impact our work because Palestine is one of the lines of work that can really impact your career, in any field, if you're not careful about how you go about advocating for this line of work. They take pictures of us, we think "What are they using those pictures for? Are they trying to figure out our names, who we are specifically?" Some of us feel as though, eyes are constantly on us.

This feeling of "eyes are constantly on us" had the effect of making activists like Ghassan nervous about people's intentions and the harm they could cause. Feeling surveilled contributed to activists being often on alert, which made them feel alone. Ghassan spent energy wondering whether he was safe given that his peers surveilled him. Because his peers with dominant identities were not surveilled, they likely did not understand how Ghassan felt, which contributed to the isolation.

Isolation sometimes meant losing people and relationships. However, even as activists lost relationships and felt isolated, some believed that these losses might be beneficial in their movement forward. McKenzie, an African American and Native woman, said:

> When you talk about something bigger than yourself, when they can't open their minds to other things, that is when you start losing people. You start to lose those certain relationships, and at the time it hurts because this person has been with me for so long. How will anybody be able to replace the support that they have given me? Everybody is not going to walk the same path with you, and sometimes, that is good, at the end of the day, because what you might be standing for they might have tried to diminish on the backend.

McKenzie conveyed the pain that stemmed from losing relationships with people with whom she had been connected for a long time. Knowing she needed to end this relationship did not necessarily soften the pain. Similarly, Madeline, a Black woman said, "I've lost a lot of connections that I thought I had with some people in my life." She continued, "I don't necessarily know whether or not to count that as a loss or gain, because I don't want people in my life who are too afraid to sacrifice a little bit for critically the good of all." Madeline's and McKenzie's experiences illustrated the loss of relationships, which could be an isolating experience. They navigated this tension knowing that some of these relationships were important to end, given they wanted people in their lives who believed in their activism and understood their experiences in their minoritized identities, yet they also noted the ways this contributed to their isolation.

Administrators and peers viewing activists as a spokesperson or representative for their minoritized identity group also contributed to activists' isolation. Danielle, a Black, straight woman, said:

> People are going to look at you entirely differently because they see you as someone who's always fired up, who gets very serious and intense about stuff. People always turn to you, turn the mic to you, whenever something absolutely painful happens whether or not you're even ready to talk about that issue yourself.

Not always wanting to speak, Danielle illustrated how she rarely had a choice in being the spokesperson. Like Danielle, Janet also became the spokesperson for her minoritized identity:

> At the beginning of a lot of classes, they'll [faculty] do the whole, "What's your name? What's your major? What's one fun fact about you? What's one organization you're involved in?" I would just casually say, "I'm involved in this LGBT organization." I became the lesbian of the class. I literally had a teacher once say, "Okay, let's get the lesbian opinion." Even if you're saying this sort of tongue in cheek, that's not appropriate at all for class. I often felt

> very singled out in that way in the classroom. There was a joke at one point that I was the most visible lesbian on campus, because I ended up winning an award for the activism. Being that visible, I guess, was a thing that caused a little bit of backlash.

Being seen as the spokesperson had the effect of furthering the isolation they already felt as activists. Treating someone as a spokesperson presumed the student was able to speak on behalf of all members of their minoritized group, and since they could not, this expectation put pressure on the student to represent the group in the correct ways. Because students could not possibly represent their entire group, treating them as such isolated them from their minoritized peers, as it positioned them as exceptional or tokens (who cannot have any flaws) as compared to their peers. Rachel, a white, straight woman, talked about the volume of people who needed her: "Then the third layer of it would be the sheer amount of people that came to me, and not feeling like I had any downtime." This expectation that activists needed to engage with people was an isolating experience and did not allow them space to recuperate in the midst of their activism.

Emotional Trauma

In Chapter 3, we discussed key concepts important for understanding the needs of student activists and how to support them. One of those concepts, racial battle fatigue (i.e., the mental, physical, and emotional consequences that come from continued exposure to racism), closely relates to the idea of emotional trauma, which many students in our study described. Given the labor activists performed for their institutions, student activists discussed feeling emotionally, physically, and mentally exhausted. Activism took a toll on their bodies and minds, resulting in emotional trauma. Amber, a Black, straight woman, talked about feeling drained as a result of her activism: "I remember always feeling exhausted, not really mentally [exhausted] because my classes were not hard at all but emotionally exhausted from being that person all the time because there were no other Black people in my classroom." Amber described her emotional exhaustion due to navigating activism as the only Black person in her classes. "I think in any activist circle," Marie, a white lesbian woman, added, "you find you get a lot of burnout. You get really tired, you're tired of being the voice, you're tired of putting all this energy when there's not a lot of thanks given back to it." Activists like Marie experienced burnout because rarely did others give to them in the ways they gave to their institutions. Averi talked about experiencing depression from her activism:

> I was very depressed. I was very much hurting. I was in a place where I felt this, as well as my friends that I was connecting to that were not around me because I wasn't there physically with them. There was a lot of concern that if I stayed any longer at [institution], I would not be able to survive.

Burnout and depression were serious health consequences for activists that affected their emotional well-being as college students (Gorski, 2018; Vaccaro & Mena, 2011).

Because some student activists hold minoritized identities, they often addressed issues directly related to their survival. A white genderqueer person, Lucia, underscored the personal nature of their activism, "To understand my gender the way that it is makes talking about gender identities, or gender minorities, it makes it more personal, which means it can sometimes take more emotional resources to talk about." As a genderqueer person, talking about their identities was personal, which led to Lucia needing more emotional resources to engage in activism around gender. Other activists highlighted the emotional toll of their activism. Scarlet, a white bisexual woman, shared one such example: "It's a very emotional thing [engaging in activism]. There's definitely a lot of emotional cost involved with it [such as] time and energy." Similarly, Janet noted:

> There's emotional toll within the community when, a lot of times, our tendency is not to build each other up; it's to tear each other down. That's an emotional toll because you think, "That's the people I'm supposed to be getting support from."

Janet continued, commenting on the emotionally taxing nature of not getting support from those who she believed should offer support, given some shared identities:

> When I ceased to be in that specific organization even though I'd given years to it, I had people who were viciously attacking me, saying, "Ding dong, the witch is dead. I'm so glad that she's out of this. Now, we can do whatever we want to do," as if I was really the impediment. That was something that was really difficult.

Needing to practice self-care and remove herself from an organization that was hurting her emotionally, Janet did so, and in the process, her exit was even more emotionally draining.

Marie lessened her activism due to health problems:

> Activism is very taxing emotionally, just because you're not getting paid for it, and you're putting in so much work. I've kind of taken a back-burner on [student organization name] this year just because I'm a senior, and I need to get my life together. I would literally spend 30 hours a week, sometimes, just planning, getting things together, spending my own money, making sure this organization succeeded and that people were turning up to events, people are happy, you know. That was really hard on my emotional health

> and also my grades as well. I'm a good student, I think that if I wasn't doing it I think I would do better. But that's kind of the sacrifice that I made, and I decided this is what I'm going to put to the forefront, and I'm going to share the forefront.

Marie noted how her emotional health suffered as a result of her activism, describing her activism as a sacrifice she made, in part because it was unpaid. Spending a significant amount of time in activism had costs.

Participants also noted how exposure to stories of oppression impacted emotional trauma. Rachel shared one such example related to sexual violence:

> The first source of exhaustion that comes is just the systematic stress of having been through the experience yourself and then hearing it re-lived through someone else's story; the details may be different, but at the end of the day, you're both victims of the same crime. Just feeling re-traumatized by that. They call that vicarious trauma, to where you start to feel your own pain come back through someone else's experience.

Vicarious trauma (Vaccaro & Mena, 2011) was a real experience among participants and impacted their own trauma. Consistently hearing stories of "the same crime" had the effect of added stress.

Given the oppression activists experienced, some sought ways to heal; however, doing so was often challenging, as Marie discussed:

> There's not a lot of mental health resources; that would be definitely something negative attached to being an activist. You have to be careful; you have to learn how to do self-care and learn how to step away and say no to things right from the get-go.

Marie noted not having access to mental health resources to process the emotional labor of her activism. Other activists, like Jason, a straight Black man, commented that even when they had access, sometimes counselors did not understand how to work with activists:

> When counselors receive people going through those struggles, and they don't understand the type of fatigue, the type of frustration, the type of pain that's experienced within the communities that they don't relate to, then it adds to the trauma that those communities are experiencing.

Activists noted how they experienced emotional trauma as a result of their activism, and yet, they had few resources to help them navigate oppression and work to heal from their trauma.

Schoolwork Suffering

In the previous section, Marie noted how her activism impacted her academics, given inadequate time to focus on her schoolwork. In this section, we share further examples of a significant cost of activism on participants' academic learning and performance. When sharing about her activism, Jamie, a white bisexual woman, said, "Trying to balance self-care and activism is something that I need to get better at; otherwise, I'm going to burn out or even not graduate." Expanding further on her comments, Jamie continued, "There's been some failures as far as working out a schedule to make sure my classwork still gets done and I'm able to make this meeting and work." Balancing activism with coursework was challenging for Jamie, and she often worried about graduating due to prioritizing her activism.

Although Jamie mentioned concern with her schoolwork, Marie talked about actually failing courses as a result of her activism: "There was a lot of burnout, and I just got so stressed to the point where I started failing classes. I was talking about empathy and being joyful in communities, and I didn't feel that at all." Participants mentioned just not having time to devote to their academics. As an Asian, queer, genderqueer person, Zi said, "One of the biggest downsides of the way that I've engaged with student life and activism is that it's a lot of time that I'm not spending studying." Not spending time on academics meant activists often did not have the "privilege of just being students," to reference Teresa's comment from earlier.

Because activists also hold many minoritized identities, they experienced consequences related to their academics that were also tied to their minoritized identities. Activists with more dominant identities (e.g., a white, heterosexual, cisgender man) likely did not experience marginalization in classroom spaces. Thus, having minoritized identities as activists was an added layer for the kind of trauma they might experience in classroom spaces, which impacted their academics. For example, Jason, referencing his Black subordinated racial identity, said the following:

> With group projects, students, their perspectives, aren't valued. They're marginalized and then when conflict happens within that marginalization, the professors are more likely to listen to the white students than the Black student who's being marginalized. Then their grades are put in jeopardy, and a lot of those students are on scholarship as well. They can potentially lose their scholarship, so that process silences them.

Activists did not have the privilege of just being students; they engaged in activism to address oppression, and as a result, for some, their academic performance suffered.

Takeaways From Seeing Student Activism as Labor

Student activists we interviewed shared in great detail, and often emotionally, about the sheer exhaustion from engaging in activism. The extra labor they performed absolved administrators of doing their jobs and working to address oppression. Students desired to just be students but felt compelled to become activists due to oppression on their campuses and working to exist freely in their minoritized identities. Activists discussed three specific ways their labor impacted them: they felt isolated; they experienced emotional trauma; and their schoolwork suffered. In this section, we discuss three larger conclusions we want readers to take from student activists' labor. First, we return to the notion of labor and discuss why examining labor critically has important implications for working with student activists. Next, we draw larger meaning from the costs of isolation and vicarious trauma. We then conclude with how institutions benefit from activists' labor.

Whose Labor Is Rewarded?

Student activism is a form of labor; activists engage in work to improve their campuses in a variety of ways. For example, the student activists described their experiences calling attention to oppression on campus through awareness-raising events and writing demands to campus administrators. They described educating peers in and out of classrooms around issues of power, privilege, and oppression. They also described supporting their peers experiencing trauma. They are rarely compensated for any of this work. In fact, much of the work that student activists engage in is similar to the work that campus staff members are trained and paid to do. Although student activists experience some growth and learning, described as cultivating wisdom in Chapter 4, as a result of their activism, the costs and consequences of their engagement may not outweigh the benefits. Further, campus officials pride themselves on creating opportunities for students' growth and development; if student activists did not have to engage in the ongoing labor to make their campuses better, they might be able to engage more fully in the opportunities provided by faculty and staff on their campuses.

Activists' title of *student* puts them in a precarious position. On the one hand, they are students working to learn, develop, and graduate from college; on the other hand, they are activists working to live more freely in their bodies and address oppression. Administrators see their activism as a choice and therefore not necessarily something for which they should be compensated. Administrators financially compensate students for doing work in other ways (e.g., working as a resident assistant, working in a campus dining hall). The problem is that administrators often do not see activists as making their campuses better, but as troublemakers; yet, administrators are unwilling to take on activists' labor in addressing oppression institutionally. Similarly, supervisors of administrators with minoritized identities often make them feel that they should not engage in this kind of identity-based labor (see Linder, Evans, Quaye, Lange, & Stewart, 2019), as identity-based labor often pushes against systems of oppression by holding institutions accountable for not living up to their espoused values around equity and inclusion. Student activists do not catalog their hours doing this kind of labor;

they are not salaried employees; they do not have performance evaluations, which makes their activism tricky to measure.

Let us be clear—we do not advocate that administrators simply pay student activists for their labor, believing that would resolve the issue. The solution is not simply to pay them and move on. Instead, we advise that those paid by the institution take on this labor to enable activists to just be students. We want the labor to shift to administrators and educators, who hold more formal and informal power than students. Activists often negotiated the choice to engage in activism, which often felt like a false choice. They could decide to focus on being a student and not engage in activism, but they often felt responsible to their communities and were navigating institutional and systemic oppression, which necessitated responding in order to survive as minoritized activists.

The Cost of Isolation and Vicarious Trauma

Student activists also discussed the isolation they experienced from their activism. They lost friendships and often did not feel supported in their activism. Although some students seemed to have peace over losing some relationships, their narratives reveal the taxing nature of losing that support. The isolation they experienced exacerbated their labor, as they did not have people with whom to commiserate about their struggles.

Participants' stories further indicate that isolation materialized in their experience when they were asked or assumed to be a spokesperson for their entire identity group. This put pressure on activists to represent their group appropriately and did not allow them space to have flaws. Being a spokesperson also had consequences around being called pejorative names (e.g., one participant indicated being called a "race warrior"), which had the effect of further isolating activists from their peers. Because their peers and administrators saw activists as exceptional or special, they did not empathize with these feelings of loneliness. Activists discussed feeling repeatedly monitored, knowing their actions had consequences for their minoritized group. This feeling of being monitored contributed to more labor on their part by feeling emotionally taxed.

Participants also noted the effects of vicarious trauma (Vaccaro & Mena, 2011), where hearing stories of trauma made them experience second-hand trauma or re-live their own trauma. Given their activism, they often listened to stories from their peers about their oppression. Hearing these stories over and over again led to them experiencing additional trauma by reflecting on these stories in relation to their own oppression. One might read this and believe activists need to seek counseling as a way to heal. Many of them did, and still, they were often paired with counselors who minimized their experience or did not understand the severity of what they were expressing given different social identities.

Institutional Benefits of Activism

Institutions benefit from student activism in a variety of ways, some implicitly, some explicitly. We explore how institutions benefit from the co-optation of student activism, as well as student activists providing a form of campus climate assessment for them.

Co-optation of Student Movements

One important way institutions benefit from identity-based activists' labor is that they can use student movements to their benefit when convenient for them. Critical race theorists refer to this as interest convergence, an idea that illustrates how white people only address racism when they see how doing so benefits their own interests (Bell, 1980; Delgado & Stefancic, 2001; Patton, 2016). Similarly, institutional leaders are motivated to change when it benefits them politically, financially, or institutionally. Their interests do not center on addressing racism because it is the right thing to do given the pernicious ways it impacts People of Color; they address it because there is some benefit to their dominance. As such, institutions have the luxury of remaining unchanged until activists bring attention to an issue, and then determining whether and how they should respond given how their own interests merge with activists' needs.

For example, institutional leaders must work to ensure the institution has a positive reputation, so when students do the labor of raising awareness about racism, sexism, and other forms of oppression on campus, institutional leaders may capitalize on this work to denounce oppression, without doing any actual work to dismantle oppression. When students raise awareness about overt racism on campus, university presidents often issue a statement indicating that the campus does not tolerate racism, yet take no other action to address racism in institutional structures and practices (Cole & Harper, 2017). Therefore, institutions gain the benefit of appearing to support anti-racism without really shifting any policies or practices to actually interrupt racism.

When activists raise concerns related to oppression, administrators often only hear the activists when they see a benefit to the institution or to them politically. This benefit illustrates how change often happens; people in positions of power, primarily white men, get to determine the pace of progress. They sometimes stall progress as a tactic until they see how the progress will also benefit them and the larger institution.

At times, institutional leaders may co-opt student movements for their own benefit, thereby diminishing the strength of the activism. When movements become institutionalized, they often lose their radical edge (Ferguson, 2017). Movements related to sexual violence provide an illustration of this challenge. Student activists have been organizing to address issues of sexual violence on campus for decades—and activists in larger communities have been organizing for centuries (McGuire, 2010). For decades, advocates and women's center staff have provided support to survivors of sexual violence in the aftermath of sexual violence. As student activists organized to advocate for more university accountability related to sexual violence, many of the services previously provided in women's centers moved to health and counseling centers and Title IX offices. In this move to more institutional accountability, many of the services focus more on legal and criminal justice processes than on survivor-centered healing and empowerment. In many cases, the co-optation of grassroots activism in women's centers to more formal institutional structures results in weakened services for survivors.

Informal Campus Climate Assessments

A second way institutions benefit from activists' labor is through informal campus climate assessments. Activists are astute in knowing how the institution is operating and where gaps exist in offerings and support. Through expressing how they experience oppression, they can point out where the institution fails to create an environment conducive to their needs. Because most institutions center an appreciation for diversity and social justice in their mission statements, not creating environments where students with minoritized identities can learn in an environment free of oppression and trauma means they are not living up to their promises in mission statements. Rather than having to perform campus climate assessments, institutions benefit from free assessments, so to speak, from activists who point out problems with the campus climate. Thus, activists serve as auditors of campuses, noting places to "fix" to improve their experiences.

Further, administrators often feel compelled to respond to activists' demands to reduce negative publicity. Although some may assume that negative publicity might reduce prospective student interest in the institution, other students (namely those with minoritized identities) might be more willing to attend an institution where student activism is prominent, as it means campus administrators are made aware of their needs and they see students who are also committed to working to address those needs. On the other hand, given the toll that activism takes on students, students might exhaust themselves to the point where they drop out of the institution, and thus, the "problem" goes away, thereby, benefiting administrators who see activists as troublemakers.

Conclusion

Student activists with minoritized identities work tirelessly to hold their institutions accountable for addressing racism, sexism, homophobia, and other systemic issues that impact their experiences as students. Given their minoritized identities, they often do not have the luxury of just being students but feel compelled to name and address oppression so that they, and their peers, can live more freely in their bodies. In this chapter, we illustrated how student activism manifests as a form of unpaid labor, which has significant costs to activists while also benefiting the institution in important ways. In the next chapter, we discuss student activists' relationships with administrators.

References

Bell, D. A., Jr. (1980). *Brown v. Board of education* and the interest-convergence dilemma. *Harvard Law Review, 93*(3), 518–533. doi:10.2307/1340546

Cole, E. R., & Harper, S. R. (2017). Race and rhetoric: An analysis of college presidents' statements on campus racial incidents. *Journal of Diversity in Higher Education, 10*(4), 318–333.

Delgado, R., & Stefancic, J. (2001). *Critical race theory: An introduction*. New York, NY: New York University Press.

Ferguson, R. A. (2017). *We demand: The university and student protests*. Oakland, CA: University of California Press.

Gorski, P. (2018). Racial battle fatigue and activist burnout in racial justice activists of color at predominantly white colleges and universities. *Race, Ethnicity and Education*. Epub ahead of print 18 July 2018. doi:10.1080/13613324.2018.1497966

Linder, C., Evans, M. E., Quaye, S. J., Lange, A. C., & Stewart, T. J. (2019, March 4). "*You hired me to do this": Power, identity, and educators' support of student activists*. Paper presented at the annual meeting of ACPA: College Student Educators International, Boston, MA.

Linder, C., Quaye, S. J., Lange, A. C., Roberts, R. E., Lacy, M. C., & Okello, W. K. (2019). "A student should have the privilege of just being a student": Student activism as labor. *The Review of Higher Education, 42*, 37–62.

McGuire, D. L. (2010). *At the dark end of the street: Black women, rape, and resistance—a new history of the civil rights movement from Rosa Parks to the rise of black power*. New York, NY: Alfred A. Knopf.

Patton, L. D. (2016). Disrupting postsecondary prose: Toward a critical race theory of higher education. *Urban Education, 51*(3), 315–342.

Pierce, J. L. (1996). *Gender trials: Emotional lives in contemporary law firms*. Berkeley, CA: University of California Press.

Vaccaro, A., & Mena, J. A. (2011). It's not burnout, it's more: Queer college activists of color and mental health. *Journal of Gay & Lesbian Mental Health, 15*(4), 339–367. doi:10.1080/19359705.2011.600656

6

STUDENT ACTIVISTS' RELATIONSHIPS WITH EDUCATORS AND ADMINISTRATORS

As the landscape of higher education has changed over time, so too have students' relationships with educators and administrators on college and university campuses. In this chapter, we explore the relationships between student activists and educators and administrators, utilizing multiples sources of evidence and triangulating elements from prior literature, our lived experiences, and interview data from 25 student activists and 17 campus educators. We interviewed educators identified as supportive by student activists in our study. Student expectations for support were low, as many of the student activists demonstrated a strong understanding of the nuances of power on campus, yet identified educators as supportive when they provided the bare minimum of potential support for their work. Additionally, student activists astutely noted when educators and administrators placated, gaslit, or ignored them. Further, student activists holding minoritized identities found themselves teaching the educators and administrators who were supposed to be serving as support.

Like students, many educators, particularly those holding minoritized identities, experienced challenges navigating institutional politics. Specifically, educators and students alike noted that pre-tenure faculty and staff with minoritized identities, including those who worked in identity-based centers, did not always have the luxury of speaking out as they wanted. Students also noted that educators and administrators with more formal power hid behind policy and politics as a strategy for not implementing what the students needed.

In the following sections, we first discuss experiences that student activists shared that complicate their relationships with educators and administrators. Supportive educators often further triangulated students' frustrating experiences with administrators on their campuses. Then, we employ stories from educators to illuminate two common barriers they face that impact the ways they show up for student activists. We conclude with a call to action for educators and administrators regarding their support for identity-based student activists.

Student Activists' Experiences

In this section, we amplify the voices of student activists to tell the story of the complicated relationships they have with educators and administrators. Student activists have very low expectations of people who work on campuses; yet even with their low expectations, they still experience troublesome interactions with educators and administrators. Identity, positionality, type of activism, and institutional type created nuance in the experiences of identity-based student activists when interacting with educators. The themes we illustrate in this section include placating and "waiting out" student activists; gaslighting; perpetuating a troublemaker trope; and protecting the institution, program, or department.

Placating and "Waiting Out" Student Activists

As a strategy to avoid creating real change on college and university campuses, students pointed out that many educators and administrators placated activists in a variety of ways. Some administrators attempted to please activists by giving in to some of their demands, but not all, and others responded paternalistically, making activists feel as though they exaggerated their experiences with hostile campus climates. Additionally, student activists noted the ways administrators exhausted or waited them out so that they did not have to address activists' concerns.

Danielle, a Black woman undergraduate student, effectively captured one experience of placating from administrators:

> We [student activists] have had the experience of feeling babied. The experience of feeling like if we come to the university administration with an issue, they give us a response that's just designed to placate us. It's designed to just shut us up for a time being.

Danielle explicitly stated that administrators give her placating responses that are intended to push her concerns aside. Placating responses include actions like initiating task forces with no real intention of making change or keeping people busy with writing diversity strategic plans or statements until the activists graduate or give up from pure exhaustion. Jason, a Black gay man, shared another example of administrators placating students:

> I think oftentimes administrators use very kind terms like, "Wow, you're very intelligent," or things like, "I never really thought about that," or things like, "Can you tell me more about your experience?" I see them feigning ignorance. I see that happening to me personally. I love meeting with

> administrators because the first thing they'll do, they'll give you this short ass meeting, like 15 or 30 minutes and then they'll start off the conversation with some shit like, "How's your day going?" They'll try to have informal conversation and drag out that conversation until the 11th hour, until you get to the point of talking about the issue and then it's like, "Oh you know what, we're out of time. We're going to have to reschedule." I see that happening a lot.

Jason offered another way that administrators placated students: administrators meet with the students, but then use the limited time to pretend to not know about the students' issues or to engage in informal conversation as a way to not address their concerns, rather than learning about the students' concerns.

Student activists noted how educators waited them out, letting undue time pass in the hopes that busy, overburdened students will forget or give up on the change they desired to see. Teresa, a Latina undergraduate student activist, shared:

> [Educators are] just tiring people out, so I think that that's a strategy that they use, I genuinely believe that they, "Oh, let's work on this." And then a month from now, students graduate, students get tired, students worry about their own things, and then they don't have to do it anymore.

Teresa went on to say that some educators on her campus also felt justified in using blatant lies to appease students: "[S]aying that they've resolved an issue, but then not actually doing so." Telling Teresa her issue was important and warranted resolution while failing to even engage with it caused more harm than good. Students were savvier than many administrators believed and, like Teresa, could see through appeasement.

Jamie, a white bisexual woman undergraduate student, conveyed a similar point about waiting students out: "Once the people who were there when the original injustice happened are gone, the people who are left have been so normalized to the situation that they might not be putting up as much of a fight." As Jamie described, waiting out students had the intended effect—it exhausted activists to the point where they no longer had the energy to fight the issue, capitalizing on students' labor. Zi, a genderqueer Asian student, shared their experiences trying to connect with administrators on their campus:

> There's just so much symbology around this [the ability to connect with administration]. The administration building at [institution] is ten stories tall and is the tallest building on our campus, and the president works at the very top of that building. I think that's just very fitting of the experience of administrators . . . I will be meeting on Monday with our Dean of Academic Affairs. He doesn't meet with students on a regular basis. He meets with students maybe 12 to 14 times a semester, which is better than some

> other administrators, but I feel like it's really easy for people at the top of that hierarchy to forget that students are people and to start thinking about them as numbers.

With the lack of connection came a lack of validation or even an opportunity to engage with the administration in a way that affirmed students' experiences. Marie, a lesbian undergraduate student who engaged in queer activism on her campus and served as the student government diversity representative, said that getting in touch with administrators was a feat in itself, and when she was able to connect with administrators strategically, they ignored her concerns:

> When we address concerns towards the administration, it's just like yelling into the void, and there's not much back. Even if we were to go to undergraduate student government and talk to the administrators that come in and visit the [student] senate, it would be just, like, "Oh I hear you," and then they would just continue forward with what they were going to do anyway.

Although Marie assumed that administrators would placate her, her assumptions were grounded in her previous experiences with administrators. Without adequate communication, Marie would never know what steps administrators took or did not take, which may result in feelings of invalidation. Closely related to placating responses includes gaslighting, which we explore in the next section.

Gaslighting

Some students in our study who talked with educators or administrators experienced gaslighting, which describes strategies used to make people who are experiencing trauma or oppression believe they are "crazy" or imagining that what they are experiencing is not real (Abramson, 2014). Alyssa, an Asian American undergraduate student activist who shared that she had a positive relationship with campus administrators, said that at times, she felt like educators, particularly those within the institution's campus safety department, used deceptive ploy tactics with activists. For example, Alyssa shared examples of educators only offering meeting times when school was not in session or respectfully communicating with her, but referring to her friends and co-conspirators condescendingly as "those other students." She said, "It sounds very menacing the way they said it, so like, we trust you but we don't trust them. Really, they should trust all the students, so yeah a lot of subtle language was used." Pitting the students against one another, making them seem unorganized or lacking unity, is one way that educators' actions served to gaslight student activists.

Amber, a Black woman doctoral student, shared a particularly troublesome conversation she had with her teaching supervisor when she approached them about the consistent microaggressions she was experiencing within the department. In response to Amber's concerns, the teaching supervisor said, "Well, you know, 50 years ago, we wouldn't be sitting at the same table, so things are not really as bad as you think they are." Marie also shared experiences of gaslighting and recalled times that educators told her that her experiences were not as bad as she thought, again invalidating student's experiences.

Jamie recalled a conversation she had with the vice president of student affairs in which she told him that queer and trans students were feeling unsupported on campus despite the vice president and his staff using inclusive language:

> I feel like we get gaslit a fair amount. I was part of a meeting with the Vice President of Student Affairs a couple of weeks ago. We literally said we don't feel supported by the administration. You keep saying all these buzz words like diversity and reason and yada yada. Then you go and do policies that are super harmful. Exactly the opposite. The VP feigned ignorance to the policies that were causing harm to queer and trans students.
>
> He was like, what policies? I don't know what you're talking about? We literally had to lay out specific things in the past year that he knew about. He was completely aware of them. He still made us have to lay it out for him.

Experiences with gaslighting escalate based on student activists' identities. Administrators often deemed student activists who engaged in resistance or activism tied to their minoritized identities as the problem, while they frequently celebrated those who engaged from their dominant identity (Linder, 2019a). Alyssa, a Woman of Color, shared,

> I know that, for me, being a Woman of Color, speaking to middle administrators was very difficult. I think the way that men in general approach woman and mansplaining, letting them know that I knew what I was doing but then they would tell me, "Oh you haven't really experienced . . . life yet. You have a lot to learn. Let us do the work."

As shown in Alyssa's example, responses based on racism, homo/bi/transphobia, sexism, ableism, and other forms of oppression further reinforce the dominant narrative of who did the work, who held power, and who was worthy of protection.

Perpetuating a Troublemaker Trope

Similar to students' experiences with gaslighting, educators and administrators alluded to student activists as troublemakers. In fact, some educators and administrators viewed, student activists in a negative light, labeling the student activists' actions as a distraction while they deemed many of their peers' actions as leadership (Martin, 2014). This example was another way educators and administrators situated themselves as the victor or remaining on the moral high ground. If the student activists were troublemakers, then who could blame the institution for not bending to their needs? Some educators sustained the belief that student activists engage in activism without understanding the impact of their actions or without understanding the bigger picture because administrators often paint student activists' actions as going in direct opposition of the institution (Spade, 2017). Student activists who engage in activism related to one or more of their minoritized identities experienced a more strained relationship with educators because educators viewed their activism as a direct threat to the institution or institutional reputation (Linder, Quaye, Stewart, & Okello, 2017).

Educators in our study also noted that administrators viewed activism as something to be managed and viewed student activists as troublemakers. Lia, a student affairs educator working in an identity-based office, talked about her perception of administrators' take on student activism:

> They [administration] don't want troublemakers, aka student activists who . . . make the top headline on *Higher Ed Today* or on *The Chronicle*, right? . . . They're doing this because they truly love this nation, this institution and they truly want it to reflect, they want us to do better and we're not and so that's why they're protesting and they're marching and they're disrupting.

Minoritized students and educators who support minoritized students carry the burden of educating and advocating for minoritized students' needs. Our collective experiences as identity-based educators tell us that administrators often see the requests of minoritized students and their advocates as too demanding. For example, a common request from cisgender educators of LGBT resource centers is to educate those on campus about helping to create trans-inclusive spaces. While the intent is almost always good, during these educational sessions, it becomes clear that many of the questions and concerns about having trans students, staff, and faculty on campus center around the need for accommodations. Many cisgender educators and administrators view trans-inclusive accommodations as extra or special privileges, when trans folks, like all students, are simply asking for a safe and welcoming place for them to learn and engage in their studies, find community, and grow.

Pete, a genderqueer, bisexual, South Asian undergraduate student activist who engaged in queer and race-based activism, shared another example of educators painting activists as the cause of the problem, rather than acknowledging the injustice as the cause of the problem:

> I'll give an example of what institutional support doesn't look like and how that relates to what it does look like. When we first protested the events

> that were happening on campus, one of them was actually an organization like a debate team or something. They were debating whether Black Lives Matter is harmful to race relations in the United States. We protested the event and [institution] came out with a response saying, "We need to engage not enrage."

This example shows the power of the institution to dictate the public discourse around the activities of student activists. In this example, the university alluded to the fact that the student activists were inciting rage, rather than the white supremacists whose actions were at the root of the conversation. Again, if the institution could paint the activists as those who incite trouble and violence, rather than pointing to the source of violence the students were speaking against, then the institution continued to be seen as holding the moral high ground. This is not dissimilar to how the national media portrays NFL players kneeling in protest of police brutality during the national anthem or Black Lives Matter protesters peacefully shutting down a highway in protest of state-sanctioned violence against Black lives (Banks, 2018; Coombs, Lambert, Cassilo, & Humphries, 2019; Dixon, 2017). In all these examples, both on campus and off, those outside of the activism vilify the activists themselves by placing the focus on the activists' actions rather than the injustices they activists are protesting.

Protecting the Institution, Program, or Department

Another negative experience student activists described included administrators and educators working to protect the institution, program, or department's reputation or status over the needs of the students. While most educators and administrators likely would not describe it this way, students felt as though protecting the status quo was more important than protecting them. Student activists also highlighted the role of power and dominance in administrators and educators' efforts to protect the institution.

Lee, a transgender white doctoral student, shared an interaction that exemplified the ways educators and administrators contributed to maintaining the status quo and protecting institutional reputation through inaction and dismissal of the concerns of minoritized students. Lee said, "[Administrators and educators] have their role at the university, and their role is not to follow any interest of their student activists. Their role is to work in the interest of the department, the university, the program, whatever it is." Lee's statement provides a clear example of the ways campuses have failed to publicly respond to student activism particularly when it concerns systemic, institutionalized racism (Cho, 2018).

Teresa, a Latina undergraduate student, expressed a similar idea: "[Educators and administrators are] like, 'Wow, you're doing a great job,' but when it comes out like when exposing [institution] or protesting or making a disruption, I guess that taints their image, and I don't think that they appreciate that." Power is inherently part of the institutional response to student activism. Student activists have to follow procedures or processes that are put in place by the majority to protect the majority. For example, many institutions have free speech areas or zones. These areas are the only place that students are allowed to protest or publicly voice their opposition; in turn, activists cannot interrupt the flow of power without disrupting the system. Thus, institutional leaders see student activists as a threat (Hoffman & Mitchell, 2016). When educators and administrators spend more time creating policies and procedures meant to protect the institution rather than the students, student activists are left no other choice but to push back on the system.

Student activists indicated that some educators and administrators used institutional culture, policies, or positionality as a reason to only partially engage with student activists. As a way of distracting or thwarting the efforts of student activists, administrators may withhold information, resources, or expertise (Ropers-Huilman, Carwile, & Barnett, 2005). Students in our study expressed similar experiences. For example, Pete shared:

> The biggest cop out is "We [administrators] have to protect student privacy so we can't tell you what consequences students are facing because of things that they've done so we never know about accountability." So that's one of the biggest excuses. Because the fact of the matter is we know people who know those students personally, so we know nothing is happening but we just want to hear from the administration. That's their biggest cop out.

Janet offered the example of campus climate surveys as another overused institutional mechanism that frequently turned into a non-performative:

> I asked, "Okay, so what are you going to do to make life for LGBT students safer on campus?" The administrator said, "Oh, we're going to do the campus climate survey, so don't worry about it." I'm like, "Okay, you're going to do a survey about what I'm telling you right now people are feeling, and then what the survey confirms?" What have we seen since then? Nothing. To be honest, I really can't think of any administrator-level positive action that really impacted any kind of my activism.

Student activists saw the use of climate studies as a way to stall students in their activism. This stalling had the effect of exacerbating activists' labor.

After conducting a campus climate study, many administrators will convene a task force to address the concerns raised in the climate study. Unfortunately, many task forces end up being a non-performative, or a way to address an issue without really addressing it (Ahmed, 2012). Non-performatives usually result in creating busy work, such as writing reports and documents, rather than actually engaging in action that may create institutional change (Ahmed, 2012).

Part of navigating culture hinges within the systems of the culture. Institutions within a large system (i.e., state systems) are beholden, in part, to systematic policies and procedures. Astutely, Zi shared, "I feel like one of the biggest things about activism, on campuses specifically I guess, though also in political activism in general, is remembering that systems are supposed to work for you rather than you're working for the system." Here, Zi alluded to the understanding that the same systems that they and other student activists worked to push against were the same systems that many educators and administrators worked to uphold. Connectedly, another student activist, Alyssa shared, "For me, it's transformational change, so activism has to be something that tackles systems and institutions."

Partially because of the fear instilled into educators around the power and vengeance of the governing systems of their institutions, educators who feared the system either intentionally or unintentionally let that fear influence they ways they engaged with student activists. The fear experienced by educators impacted the ways they responded to student activists. Tania, a Latinx educator who worked in an identity-based office, shared that she tried to go to as many student protests and demonstrations as she could. She also shared that she feared the consequences she may receive as a result of her support:

> I try to go as much as I can but I also make sure that it's safe for me as well. I'm also very honest about it. "Hey, I have this job that pays my mortgage and there are limits to what I can and cannot do."

Tania's honesty with student activists about the consequences she must navigate may cause an unintentional negative impact on the ways students perceived consequences for their own activism. By sharing with students all that she contended with when supporting the students' activism, she may inadvertently pass her fear on to the students adding more emotional labor for the students to carry.

In referencing the fear experienced by educators and passed on to students, Scarlet, a bisexual white undergraduate woman, shared some consequences she received as a result of her activism:

> I was chastised once. I had sent an email to the [state governing board]. Then the [state governing board] contacted the dean of students. He kind of freaked out because they felt kind of threatened. They felt like I was going rogue, but it wasn't too confrontational . . . but, they [state governing board] implemented the policy that I'm very against, but that's on a [state governing board] level.

Lee recognized the power the state governing board had over their institution, believing that the state governing board had final decision or solid input on many policy decisions. Lee shared that they were perplexed by the power of the state governing board as the board seemed so ignorant to the students' lived experiences:

> People who are alums of the university but are now incredibly wealthy people . . . have no connection to the lives of students, especially working-class and middle-class students. I think that also plays a big role even at public universities, the private sector has a huge influence on what that university does.

This was another example of how those in power, such as those on the state governing board, exercised their influence to remain in positions to make decisions that impacted many and served to uphold the status quo.

The power-conscious framework asks readers to pay attention to systems and structures that benefit those with dominant identities. Our observations as educators who have supported student activists indicate that many educators are unable or unwilling to push back on their institutional governing boards, even at the urging of student activists. Educators frequently perpetuate the idea that students have more power and influence over campus culture than educators do. While systems often silenced educators' voices, educators still hold formal power over students, so the idea that students have more power and influence than educators does not hold completely true. Perpetuating a misrepresentation of power causes harm to students. Student activists with minoritized identities name power in ways that educators are often fearful of doing themselves and in ways that make their college experience more challenging.

Educators' Experiences

In addition to the challenges that students experienced, educators also experienced barriers to supporting student activists. We share barriers that educators faced not as an excuse or a response to the challenges students faced in their relationships with educators, but as a way to provide context and help readers to think more critically as they work to support identity-based student activists. The first barrier, which was most common for educators who held minoritized identities and those who worked in identity-based roles, consisted of challenges in gaining clear expectations from supervisors and administrators regarding student activist support. This lack of clarity often left educators in precarious situations and impacted their ability to show up as needed for students. The other barrier that educators faced consisted of both implicit and explicit consequences for the support of student activists. These consequences ranged from mental and physical exhaustion to a fear of losing jobs or opportunities. The culture of fear created from these potential consequences also impacted the ways in which educators were able to show up for students.

Unclear and Unwritten Expectations

Both students and educators noted that educators, specifically those with minoritized identities and/or those who worked in identity-based centers, and pre-tenure faculty did not always have the luxury of speaking out as they wanted. Educators shared that the expectations set out for them as to how to they should engage with student activists were often elusive and felt purposefully withheld. Tania, a Latinx educator at a large, public university said:

> Some of those things were in line with my job position and I was patted on the back and even promoted at times for those efforts and some of those things were not. That's where the struggle comes in supporting students. For things that are not always in line with what your institution or organization thinks is appropriate.

Educators, particularly those in identity-based roles, often experienced the resistance of institutions to their advocacy work, even as they were employed by the same institution to do the work. Educators who engaged in diversity and equity work faced challenges that educators outside of the work did not face and may be difficult to understand (Ahmed, 2012). These challenges differentiate identity-based student advocacy from other educator roles. For example, Lia, an Asian American educator who worked in an identity-based office, shared:

> Administrators have a funny way of hiring people that they want to do this work and they want to keep us in check and they're all surprised when we do something for what we were hired for. I'm like, "Why are you acting surprised? You hired me to do this work so why are you stopping me from doing this work?" So, it's a way of checks and balances. That's how they keep us in check sometimes.

Lia demonstrated a desire to do the work for which she was hired, but she ended up having to do more work to negotiate her superiors' responses to her work. This double labor, serving the student and then figuring out how to frame that support for administrators, added to the exhaustion of the educators and kept them from engaging fully with students.

Educators shared that they did not receive any explicit messaging from their supervisors regarding student activist support or advocacy. Even Jeff, a white, cisgender, male educator who identified himself as holding a lot of dominant identities and called himself "hyper-privileged," shared his worry about joining students in direct action as his supervisor had never explicitly shared the unwritten rules of support:

> I think it just is something in the back of your mind as you're working with students and you're not sure that if you showed up at a rally like that that you wouldn't be hung out to dry or that you wouldn't suffer some political

> consequences or employment consequences in some ways as a part of being in that situation.

Even the most privileged of educators, who likely experience the least consequences for their actions, thought of ways to explain their engagement with student activists. While the field of student affairs prides itself on attempting to be inclusive and welcoming of all students, it is curious that educators were left with lingering worries about their efforts to support identity-based student activists.

Taylor, a Black gay male educator who works with identity-based student organizations, said that his supervisors only verbally shared messaging regarding his student activist support and advocacy rather than through any written communication. This tactic served to protect the institution rather than the educator. It also left educators in a precarious position for when they engaged in student activism support, leaving them vulnerable to receive consequences as they did not have a written policy or procedure to support their engagement. Taylor shared:

> Obviously, nothing's going to be explicitly communicated, but I do think it is verbally communicated because I don't think that that can be on the record all the time. I've been told at respective things that I've been in, particularly with my unit, the people above us want us to sort of manage this, and . . . be careful how you use platforms, just with the culture, the environment that we work in . . . I have felt very supported there, but I do think there are very much so some indirect kind of "we don't want any attention," so support people . . . keep them quiet as opposed to supporting them to be there for them in the way that you need to be there for them.

Unwritten or withheld expectations leave educators open to receive consequences from administrators and supervisors.

Consequences of Advocacy

Educators who support and advocate for student activists choose to interrupt power systems and structures on their campuses. This advocacy often results in consequences for these educators, including job insecurity, lowered morale, and reduced resources for their work (Harrison, 2010). People who work as leaders of identity-based centers, specifically multicultural centers, and often holding multiple minoritized identities, experience the most significant consequences (Harrison, 2010). Findings from our study affirmed the additional risk for those working in identity-based spaces. Addison, a white, trans educator, shared consequences they received for both supporting student activists and showing up as "too trans" at work:

> It was heavily implied that if I didn't shape up, maybe not at the next meeting, but the meeting after, I was pretty worried about my job . . . so, I did

> what I needed to do which wasn't necessarily stopping to support activism or stop being "more trans" but I gave that impression to her. Which is something it kind of hurt me to do because I love and respect my supervisor. It felt a little deceitful, but I think that professional activists are often put in that position of, "I have to give a professional image even though that I know that professionalism is kind of b.s." I'm going to very carefully negotiate what spaces I'm in, in front of who, how I give the advice that I give. Do I say it or do I get students to say it and then say, "Oh, it's really interesting that you said that, tell me more. What do you think that idea is about," and let them develop an idea that I have shared but can't really give them. I think that that's a thing.

Addison was not the only educator who shared that they had to engage in ways that felt deceitful or devious just to be able to do the work that they were doing to support students. Tania, a Latinx woman who is a mid-level manager in an identity-based office, shared that she had a hard time reconciling a stance the university had taken with her beliefs as they related to supporting students. She said, "I think that's where a little bit of struggle comes about, when there's a conflict between I don't want to lose my job but I do want to stand up for things that I think that are important."

We found a stark difference between the ways educators working in identity-based centers, particularly those holding minoritized identities, talked about the consequences of their advocacy versus how their peers in other offices talked about their experiences with advocacy. The majority of the white, cisgender educators in our study shared that they had not experienced many, if any, significant external consequences from their engagement with student activists. Logan, a white, cisgender man, shared that while there were more tensions when he supported student activists, and it was "time consuming and sometimes emotionally draining," he experienced no direct negative consequences. Similarly, Dorothy, a white, cisgender, female upper-level administrator shared:

> It's exhaustion, but it's also the tiredness of being brave enough, and this is coming with life, maturity as well, to figure out how you insert, not you, but enough of that . . . It's coming from the sheer exhaustion of supporting so many people who are seeking how to figure out how to do this all at once. I feel like the world's been sleeping, and it woke up all at once. It's nap time is over, and people are running around, and we're supposed to help put out all the, keep everybody moving in the same direction at once. For me, having everybody woke all at once. Would have been helpful if a couple had woke up along the way. We've had some pretty complacent generations come through our institutions. Yeah, it's just tiring.

In a very telling description, Monica, a Black woman with over 25 years of experience in higher education and currently serving as a leader within an identity-based office, shared why she was not vocal about her support of students. Monica shared both the mixed messages and the perceptions of others who advocated for minoritized students on her campus, and this perception kept her from engaging in external or hyper-visible ways:

> [T]he consequences haven't been overt or maybe not even communicated. But, I think there are times when those who might be more vocal and out front are perceived as . . . not as committed to their formal role at the institution or that they might dangerous to put in leadership positions because they . . . You're just not sure how they might respond, and they might not respond in the interest of the university. Perhaps they would be more likely to represent kind of a special interest.

Some of the white educators, especially Logan and Dorothy, shared that they experienced internal consequences (e.g., exhaustion) that the Educators of Color in our study did not explicitly name. Although Educators of Color most certainly negotiate additional labor and exhaustion when supporting student activists, they may not name it as such because it is so much a part of their experience that they do not recognize it or they are not believed when they name it as labor. This phenomenon is called *cultural taxation* (Padilla, 1994, p. 26). Cultural taxation encompasses the expectation that Educators of Color will respond to whatever administrators or supervisors deem as culturally important, as administrators and supervisors believe that Educators of Color are the only ones who can respond (Padilla, 1994). Educators of Color in our study may not have mentioned the internal consequences (e.g., exhaustion) they felt while supporting student activists. This may be because Educators of Color served as mentors to those with similar racial identities all the time, yet had never seen their extra labor as *extra*. Educators of Color serve as liaisons between the institution and Communities of Color or to diffuse or troubleshoot a situation that has arisen from cultural differences. Minoritized students also rely on educators who hold like identities, often being those who work in identity-based centers, which resulted in additional labor to those educators (Harrison, 2010; Linder, 2019b). Due to the history and current context of racism and white dominance in education, white educators often failed to recognize the undo labor put on their Colleagues of Color. This did not mean that white educators could not, and frankly should not, feel exhausted as that was certainly an understandable feeling; they must, however, be aware of the labor put on to others as well.

White, male, heterosexual educator Jeff mentioned that one of the first times that he thought about consequences of his support of student activists was when students came to him to ask for his help in navigating campus structures to help pay tribute to a Black man who was killed by police officers in the city in which the university was located:

> They [student activists] came to me and asked, "How do we get the president's office to say something that's reflective of how we're feeling about

> this particular incident that took place?" I think what was challenging for me was where before I hadn't really had to think too much about the political consequences because I enjoy a lot of autonomy and a lot of trust placed in me in my position, I feel like in that situation it was harder for me to come up with steps to take knowing that possibly it could be traced back to me . . . Nothing happened to me as a result of that but I would imagine there was some irritation and I don't know if it changed the way that she [Jeff's supervisor] looked at the way I did my job at that point but that was something that happened in response to my working with students in that weird in-between space.

Jeff's story helps to illuminate the need for educators to do their own self-work, particularly around their dominant identities. Without such interrogation and thoughtful consideration of the identities held by students they support, they will continue to do harm and remain disconnected from the needs of students engaging in identity-based student activism.

Conclusion

Educators supporting identity-based student activists have set the bar of support low, and activists deserve more than educators are currently providing. Student activists shared four themes that complicate their relationships with both educators and administrators. To better understand rather than to explain away, we looked to stories from educators to illuminate two common barriers they faced that impacted the ways they showed up for student activists.

The power-conscious framework calls for educators to do their own self-work and reflection as it pertains to their dominant identities. The framework also calls for educators to critique the systems and structures in place at their institutions that continue to uphold the system against which student activists rally. Even educators who feel sufficiently adept in their understanding and engagement with social justice and equity practices must continue to participate in education, particularly involving their dominant identities, that challenge and advance their conceptualization of power.

Students should be able to look to educators for support. For that support to be real, authentic, and helpful, educators and administrators must do the work it takes to challenge the status quo. Institutions intentionally incorporate social justice policies and practices into the lived mission of the institution (DeAngelo Schuster, & Stebleton, 2016). Without having an understanding of systems and structures that impact the lives of students and know how educators show up in those systems, they harm students.

In the final chapter, we offer practical recommendations for those seeking to support identity-based activists. The chapter also offers a reflection guide to help educators and administrators think through their praxis.

References

Abramson, K. (2014). Turning up the lights on gaslighting. *Philosophical Perspectives, 28*(1), 1–30.

Ahmed, S. (2012). *On being included: Racism and diversity in institutional life*. Durham, NC: Duke University Press.

Banks, C. (2018). Disciplining black activism: Post-racial rhetoric, public memory and decorum in news media framing of the black lives matter movement. *Continuum, 32*(6), 709–720. https://doi.org/10.1080/10304312.2018.1525920

Cho, K. S. (2018). The perception of progress: Conceptualizing institutional response to student protests and activism. *The NEA Higher Education Journal*, 81–95.

Coombs, D. S., Lambert, C. A., Cassilo, D., & Humphries, Z. (2019). Flag on the play: Colin Kaepernick and the protest paradigm. *Howard Journal of Communications*, 1–20. https://doi.org/10.1080/10646175.2019.1567408

DeAngelo, L., Schuster, M. T., & Stebleton, M. J. (2016). California dreamers: Activism, identity, and empowerment among undocumented college students. *Journal of Diversity in Higher Education, 9*(3), 216–230. https://doi.org/10.1037/dhe0000023

Dixon, T. L. (2017). Good guys are still always in white? Positive change and continued misrepresentation of race and crime on local television news. *Communication Research, 44*(6), 775–792.

Harrison, L. M. (2010). Consequences and strategies student affairs professionals engage in their advocacy roles. *Journal of Student Affairs Research and Practice*, 47(2), 197–214.

Hoffman, G. D., & Mitchell, T. D. (2016). Making diversity "everyone's business": A discourse analysis of institutional responses to student activism for equity and inclusion. *Journal of Diversity in Higher Education, 9*(3), 277–289. https://doi.org/10.1037/dhe0000037

Linder, C. (2019a). Power-conscious and intersectional approaches to supporting student activists: Considerations for learning and development. *Journal of Diversity in Higher Education, 12*(1), 17–26. http://dx.doi.org/10.1037/dhe0000082

Linder, C. (2019b). Strategies for supporting student leaders as activists. In G. M. Martin, C. Linder, & B. M. Williams (Eds.), Leadership learning through activism. *New Directions for Student Leadership, 161* (pp. 89–96). San Francisco, CA: Jossey-Bass. https://doi.org/10.1002/yd.20323

Linder, C., Quaye, S. J., Stewart, T. J., & Okello, W. (2017). *The whole weight of the world on my shoulders: Power, identity, and student activism*. Paper Presented at the annual meeting of the Association for the Study of Higher Education. Houston, TX.

Martin, G. L. (2014). Understanding and improving campus climates for activists. In C. J. Broadhurst, & G. L. Martin (Eds.), *"Radical academia"? Understanding the climates for campus activists, 201* (pp. 53–67). San Francisco, CA: Jossey-Bass. https://doi.org/10.1002/he

Padilla, A. M. (1994). Ethnic minority scholars, research, and mentoring: Current and future issues. *Educational Researcher, 23*(4), 24–27.

Ropers-Huilman, B., Carwile, L., & Barnett, K. (2005). Student activists' characterizations of administrators in higher education: Perceptions of power in "the system." *The Review of Higher Education, 28*(3), 295–312.

Spade, D. (2017, February 10). Reframing faculty criticisms of student activism. *The Chronicle of Higher Education*. Retrieved from www.chronicle.com/article/Reframing-Faculty-Criticisms/239182

7

RECOMMENDATIONS FOR EDUCATORS, ADMINISTRATORS, AND FACULTY

In this book, we illustrated the experiences of students engaged in identity-based activism—the challenges they face, the wisdom they cultivate, and the strategies they employ to foment change on their campuses. We also underscored the particular ways educators, faculty, and administrators support them in their activism, as well as how, at times, they fall short in their support of activists. In this final chapter, we offer recommendations for educators, administrators, and faculty seeking to support identity-based activists. We divide these recommendations into five sections. First, we provide guidance for educators working in identity-based centers. Then, we share advice for administrators and educators who do not work in identity-based centers. Next, we offer recommendations for faculty. In the fourth section, we provide a reflection guide for educators, administrators, and faculty in supporting activists. In the final section, we share lessons we have learned from engaging in this study, writing this book, and working with student activists.

Recommendations for Educators in Identity-Based Centers

For educators working in identity-based centers (e.g., multicultural center, women's center, LGBTQ+ center), making connections through like identities is an effective way to support activists. Student activists in the present study demonstrated how shared identities with educators was one avenue for enabling them to feel supported. We do not intend to treat educators and activists with particular minoritized identities as monolithic with this recommendation, yet we also recognize that representation matters. When educators with minoritized identities share with students how they navigate institutions given their minoritized identities, students may gain ideas to consider in their resistance. Additionally, when educators with minoritized identities discuss how they connect with people across identities, activists may also learn how fostering collaborations can strengthen their activism.

Educators in identity-based centers can also help student activists understand history and use it to inform their activism. As illustrated in Chapter 2, student activism is often cyclical, with present-day students advocating for similar issues as their predecessors (Cho, 2018; Dixson, 2018). This is often due to how systemic oppression works and how postsecondary institutions work to perpetuate the status quo. Sometimes, students engage in activism without an attention to history and end up repeating the same strategies that may have not worked previously. This is not to blame students, but instead to illustrate how understanding history can enable activists to utilize different, and perhaps more effective, methods for dismantling systems of oppression. Educators in identity-based centers are uniquely positioned to understand history and can use their knowledge to work with activists. For example, knowing that previous activists demanded more Faculty of Color, educators can engage students in conversations about why their campuses might look similar to how they did in the past, helping activists engage in nuanced conversations about history. Activists might end up demanding the same changes as their predecessors, but their knowledge will be more informed through a historical lens.

What we are suggesting in the previous paragraph is consistent with the Model of Theory to Practice (Reason & Kimball, 2012), which proposes using formal theories, informal theories, institutional context, and practice to guide one's work as an educator and repeating this cycle as one gains new knowledge and information. For example, educators in identity-based centers can use their day-to-day knowledge of working with activists (i.e., informal theories), knowledge they learn in their readings (i.e., formal theories), knowledge about how their institutions work and their histories and contexts (i.e., institutional context), and application of these knowledges (i.e., practice) to work with activists. Doing this, they can identify potential barriers and gaps and use knowledge from activists to see additional barriers they might not have otherwise known. In meetings with colleagues, they can then help them understand ways to support activists in navigating these barriers and revise their approaches as necessary.

We also suggest that educators keep making their spaces available to activists. Activists in our study often commented on how these spaces were critical for providing them respite from oppression or having a place to gather to connect with other activists and strategize. As educators invite activists to use their spaces, continue listening to activists to ensure the space is reflective of what they need. For example, a space initially designed for cisgender women may not serve the current needs of a more gender-expansive identity of women in the same ways. When educators are present in the space, activists may feel seen and know educators care about them. Working with activists in these spaces to plan their activism and using historical knowledge to help them think contextually about their strategies is also effective and consistent with power-conscious approaches. This does not mean telling activists something will not work because previous activists tried a similar strategy; rather, we are advocating that identity-based educators capitalize on their institutional knowledge to help contextualize activists' strategies within a history and context.

Finally, we recommend that educators continue to engage in self-work as well as self-care in their work with activists. The terms activists use, as well as their needs, continue to morph as activists gain more nuanced and complex understanding of themselves and their needs. As such, educators' work must also change. For example, intersectionality (Crenshaw, 1989) may be a new concept since some educators began their work in identity-based centers, but currently this term is fairly ubiquitous. Therefore, understanding the importance of using intersectional frameworks in their work with activists makes educators' work more responsive to students' experiences. Tying the power-conscious framework with intersectionality may also enhance educators' work with activists, as they can now see how power manifests in systems of oppression. In the midst of working with activists, educators will likely experience exhaustion and feel alone in doing this work. Practicing self-care, even in the midst of constant requests to do more and more to support student activists, is essential for educators in identity-based centers. Rejuvenation is important to sustain this kind of work. Self-care can look like setting boundaries with activists about the care you are able to provide. Healing can be more difficult, as healing requires more sustainable strategies that tackle the root of the problem (i.e., systemic oppression) (Okello, Quaye, Allen, Carter, & Karikari, 2018; Quaye, Carter, Allen, Karikari, & Okello, 2018). Therapy with a counselor who validates appropriately and asks helpful questions can be a path toward healing. We know that power differentials exist in educators' relationships with colleagues, and still, we hope that educators in identity-based centers can tell their colleagues what they need to be able to continue doing this work.

Recommendations for Administrators and Educators

In one of our meetings about this book, we engaged in a robust conversation about the low expectations student activists have of administrators and educators. TJ, specifically, framed this by saying, "The bar is on the floor," meaning activists have low expectations for what constitutes support from administrators. Because their experiences with administrators and educators often resulted in activists navigating barriers and being frustrated by administrators not listening to their demands and validating their needs, they needed administrators and educators to just show up, literally, to their events. Activists also mentioned the significance of administrators and educators providing them water, for example, during their protests or sit-ins. If providing water and showing up matter so much to activists, it illustrates the lack of support they often get from administrators and educators.

Let us be clear—we are not minimizing or diminishing the importance of showing up. Clearly, this was important to activists. However, we do nuance showing up and suggest that administrators and educators can and should do more to support activists.

One way to do more is the share the burden of labor. Students arrive on campus with the desire to just be students; yet, those with minoritized identities are often not afforded this privilege given the oppression they experience connected to their identities. Thus, students become activists and engage in resistance in order to address this oppression and make their campus environments more conducive to their needs. Administrators, especially, hold more formal and informal power than activists, and thus, can share this labor with activists. For example, when an administrator or educator shows up at an event, they can listen, validate, and then share what they heard with their colleagues as a way to share labor and illustrate support.

Administrators and educators with dominant identities, for example, white and cisgender men, mentioned leveraging their dominance as a way to address oppression on campus. Because white administrators and educators often mirrored the identities of those in positions of power, advocating on behalf of activists with administrators and educators who shared dominant identities was one way for activists to get their needs heard and potentially met.

Another way to support activists is to translate unknown institutional structures to help activists better navigate these systems. Taylor, a gay Black educator, shared an example of what this means:

> If I were to do something that would put my job on the line, then I'm not here to support you. I think it's very important to let people know what my limits are, and what parameters have been put around me, and what my sphere of influence is, and how I can help them. With that being said, I don't necessarily think that's stifling. I think it's just being upfront. In terms of differentiating, here's my opinions on these respective things, but also this is about operating within so I can be able to be here and support you. I just think it's necessary. I think it's very important to be transparent in those ways. I'm not necessarily going to give the student information that would kind of put me or them at risk of knowing, but at the same time, being transparent in a way that is most authentic and useful to have perspective of things that are maybe happening at my level, above me, that will impact their activism.

Taylor effectively captured one way he tries to support activists. Being transparent about his limits enables activists to understand some of the institutional structures in place. Some might see Taylor's comments as an excuse, but rather, given his own minoritized identities, he is explicit about the boundaries and spheres of influence in which he exists.

Upper-level administrators should also engage in ongoing dialogue with student activists about their needs and the root of those needs. When reading lists of demands, administrators might see items such as, "increase the percentage of Black students from 4% to 10% in five years;" "hire more faculty and staff of color;" "require diversity training for all campus employees;" or "hire more counselors who understand the needs of trans and gender non-conforming students." The immediate reaction might be, "Don't students understand how impossible it is to meet these demands?!" Inviting activists into dialogue might help administrators understand the root of these demands. For example, an administrator might learn that students want to have their experiences validated and respected on campus. Although students may ultimately want and need more staff and faculty who share or understand their experiences, they may feel less overwhelmed and harmed if administrators simply validated their negative and hurtful experiences on campus while they worked toward meeting the student demands, rather than resisting them.

Further, when administrators and students come together to discuss the root of the demands, both may develop even better strategies for addressing the root of the problem. For example, if the problem is faculty committing microaggressions against students in classrooms, students might think that hiring more Black faculty and staff is the answer. Through discussions about these issues, students may come to a different conclusion. For example, another strategy for addressing microaggressions in classrooms might be to tie equity and inclusion work to faculty tenure and promotion requirements. In conversations with activists, upper-level administrators can also be more transparent about institutional decision-making. One caveat is important here—given the labor in which activists are engaged, which we discussed in Chapter 5, demanding more time from activists is tricky. As such, establishing genuine relationships with activists based on mutual benefits is one way to ensure their time is not tokenized.

Recommendations for Faculty

Student activists in our study also engaged with faculty both in the classroom and in out-of-class settings. Because of their positions on campus, faculty, especially those with tenure, hold different formal power than educators and administrators. As such, they are uniquely positioned to utilize this power and show up in bolder, more unapologetic ways in their support of activists.

In classroom spaces, faculty can support activists by including readings that reflect multidimensional and intersectional lenses. Student activists in our study talked about often being the only person with a particular minoritized identity in the classroom space, how isolating this experience was, and the pressure to be the spokesperson for their identity. By relying upon readings that reflect the experiences of people with minoritized identities, faculty remove the onus from activists in needing to be the person who educates their peers about their experiences or feeling singled out. Faculty should be prepared to engage meaningfully with these readings to explore their unique contributions and not see these readings as outliers or exceptional.

In addition, faculty can work alongside activists in more visible ways given the power they hold in their roles as faculty. This means showing up to activists' events and supporting them publicly. Activists do not desire faculty to take over, but instead, to support them in their efforts. An additional way for faculty to show up is to collaborate with educators and administrators. Faculty can engage in conversations with educators and administrators so that all three groups can work in tandem to support activists. Because activists work in varied spaces and with various people, working jointly has potential to better meet their holistic needs.

Given that student activists sometimes struggled to balance the demands of coursework with their activism, another strategy faculty may consider is incorporating student activism into their courses. Faculty may support student activists by providing academic credit for the activism students already engage in through independent study credits. Further, many faculty members allow students to choose their topics for presentations, papers, or projects. Faculty may consider encouraging student activists to connect their activism to these projects or adjusting assignments to allow students to get credit for their work outside the classroom in the classroom.

In Chapter 5, Averi shared how participating in our study took time away from her being able to spend that time in different ways (e.g., practicing self-care). Therefore, faculty engaged in research on student activism (including ourselves) must be mindful of asking activists to spend more free labor in serving as study participants and consider potential benefits to activists of their participation.

Activists also discussed losing support from their advisors who opposed their activism. This loss of support was especially troubling given the power faculty hold in writing letters of recommendation and engaging in informal conversations with colleagues at other institutions about particular students. We advise faculty to not withhold support as a way to penalize students for their activism. Doing so is an abuse of power and reinforces barriers that activists, who are already engaged in labor, must navigate.

Finally, faculty can engage in open and transparent conversations with activists about systems of oppression and how they manifest at their particular campuses. Faculty often have knowledge about how their institutions work and can serve as conduits between activists and these systems by sharing knowledge openly and being transparent about how these structures work.

A Guide for Supporting Activists

Having offered specific advice to educators, administrators, and faculty, in this section, we offer a self-reflection guide for those wishing to support identity-based student activists. This guide is not intended to be a panacea or best practices for supporting activists; readers should consider their own strengths and limitations in the process, as well as the particular needs of activists on their campuses.

Reflect on Social Identities

How educators, administrators, and faculty support student activists is tied to their social identities. As such, reflecting on one's own dominant and subordinated identities is vital. As the power-conscious framework (see Chapter 1) reminds readers, power is always present in interactions between people, even when people do not acknowledge power. Because educators, administrators, and faculty hold more formal, and often informal, power than students, reflecting on their dominant and subordinated identities is important. Those who hold more dominant identities are better positioned to support activists more boldly, as there are fewer consequences in their public support (McElderry & Hernandez Rivera, 2017). For people who hold more minoritized identities, reflecting on those minoritized identities can be healing, enabling them to be more whole and effective in their work. However, reflecting solely on those minoritized identities is insufficient, as dominance also matters and plays a role in one's work with activists. Paying attention only to one's minoritized race means they miss seeing how their privilege as cisgender, non-disabled men, for example, prompts them to overlook or minimize the significance of sexism or ableism impacting activists' experiences.

Name Assumptions

People wishing to support activists must name and interrogate their assumptions. Questions to consider are:

- What are your assumptions about student activists?
- Do you see student activists as troublemakers?
- Who are the activists on your campus?
- To what extent do you privilege traditional leadership opportunities (e.g., service-learning, civic engagement) in which students engage?

Noting one's answers to these questions is important for understanding how one engages with activists. For instance, seeing activists as troublemakers means one will likely impede their activism, and privileging civic engagement means one may devalue the work of activists. By interrogating one's assumptions, one is better positioned to change their assumptions and hold beliefs that are more attuned to supporting activists.

Consider Context

Context matters, and where one is situated has implications for supporting activists. Institutional type and status matter. For example, working at a minority-serving institution, which has a greater percentage of students with minoritized racial identities, requires different kinds of support than historically white institutions. Additionally, local, state, and national context matter. The institutions within and near Ferguson, Baltimore, and Charlottesville all had particular local effects that came on campus (Beckett, 2018; Dixson, 2018). Zooming out further, the needs of undocumented students are likely more pronounced in certain states than others, particularly as they relate to access and aid (e.g., Reich & Barth, 2010). Paying attention to one's context means not treating all activists the same, but instead seeing how one's environment has implications for activists' experiences and needs.

Pay Attention to Historical Patterns

Just as context matters, so too does history. As seen in Chapter 2, activism has a long history with progress and setbacks. Ahistorical approaches to supporting activists result in ineffective support and run the risk of further perpetuating oppression and harming activists (Linder, 2018). Educators should understand the history of how their campuses were founded, as well as how the spaces activists use were founded (e.g., multicultural centers, queer center, disability resource center) in order to work more effectively with activists. For instance, Black student activists continue to issue the same demands their predecessors named decades ago (Bradley, 2016; Patton, 2015). Some educators and administrators might display shock at activists asking for change through a list of demands; however, it is clear that these students continue to see the institution as not being supportive of them. Paying attention to students' lists of demands over time can enable educators, administrators, and faculty to see how institutions have not lived up to their missions while giving administrators, educators, and faculty a tangible way to discuss the historical evolution of students' concerns.

Listen and Validate

Simply put, listen to *and* validate activists (Curtis, 2018). Their position as students uniquely positions them to understand the inner workings of their institutions. Even if one disagrees with activists' strategies, listening and validating are important. Activists in the present study wanted to be heard, to feel like their voices mattered. Previously, we discussed the importance of working to understand the root of activists' demands. Yes, perhaps they desire hiring more Faculty of Color so they see people who look like them in positions of power. Or, they may want more counselors who understand the needs of trans and gender-non-conforming people. These, however, are the outcomes of their demands. Listening and validating means one might understand the root of their concerns. Often, the root issue is not feeling seen or heard. By not only listening, but also validating, it illustrates that educators, faculty, and administrators are working to truly understand the needs of student activists.

Resist the Urge to Become Defensive

When listening to activists, we recognize it is likely difficult to hear activists underscore the ways administrators, educators, and faculty have not supported them; feeling like one failed in their role can lead to anger, guilt, shame, or shutting down. Activists' words can likely foster defensiveness and resistance among faculty, administrators, and educators. These actions only serve to further isolate activists, who are already in a precarious position given their lack of formal and informal power. Resisting the urge to become defensive can enable activists to feel further supported and that their needs matter. For example, if one is immediately feeling defensive, reflecting on from where that defensiveness is coming is important. Being attuned to one's feelings can help one to pay attention to when emotions surface and be able to potentially see from where the emotion is stemming.

Engage Spheres of Influence

Given their closeness to activists, some educators, administrators, and faculty have important insights to share with colleagues about ways to support activists. Administrators and educators in positions of power can leverage this power to share feedback with colleagues about what activists need. Educators in identity-based centers can work with colleagues who also have minoritized identities to engage their circles of influence. Faculty can work with department chairs and deans to share the needs of activists. Engaging with people in one's spheres of influence has potential to shift some of the onus from students to people with more power.

Attend to Systems, Not Just Individuals

Racism, sexism, white supremacy, homophobia, and the like are systemic issues. Trying to combat systemic issues with individual strategies can result in only addressing the symptoms, not the root of the issue. Individual strategies matter, and we also suggest that people work to focus on systems as well. For example, hiring more Faculty and Staff of Color without changing systemic oppression does not make the environment more conducive to them succeeding; it only addresses the symptom and not the root of the problem. Similarly, hiring more counselors to respond to the needs of trans activists without addressing genderism places these counselors in precarious positions.

Concluding Comments: Lessons Learned

We embarked on this journey to understand the needs of student activists and how to better support them because of our own experiences working with activists and engaging in activism and resistance. In writing this book, we have learned more about ourselves, and we know there will continue to be a need for activism given the ubiquity of oppression. We close this book with sharing what we have learned from our study and our own work with activists or how writing this book has impacted us.

Chris

Despite their experiences with pain, hurt, and marginalization perpetuated by institutional structures and institutional agents, minoritized student activists engage in activism out of a love for their institutions. They want the institutions to be better, so they engage in labor to try to make this happen. Identity-based student activists are resilient and wise, and we must listen to them. However, we must not take advantage of their love and labor. For most identity-based student activists, engaging in activism does not feel like a choice—rather, it feels like a responsibility or burden that they must engage to make the campus environment better for themselves and for the students who come after them. As administrators, educators, and faculty, we often take this additional labor for granted. We capitalize on students' desire for a better environment and push them to do more and more labor on behalf of the institution.

Although student activists indicate that they do learn and grow as a result of participating in activism, I question whether those benefits outweigh the costs of activism. Some activists report that they struggle to engage in traditionally academic experiences like coursework, research with faculty, and even doing their homework because of the time they spend trying to make the institution more hospitable for themselves and their peers. As a former student affairs educator, I always took pride in the level of engagement of the student activists with whom I worked and now I question that. What does it mean that we rely on student activists to do much of the work of creating equitable campus climates? How do we find the balance between asking students what they need to be successful, yet not over-relying on them to do the work that we have been hired to do?

Moving forward, I will change several things about the ways I engage around identity-based student activism. First, throughout my classes in higher education and student affairs, I will explore ideas of student activism as labor with student affairs educators. We will wrestle with the tension of listening to students about their needs and the reality that asking them to reflect on their experiences and come up with ideas about how to improve the climate is additional labor on them.

Second, I will be more mindful of the ways asking students, especially minoritized students, to participate in research studies is a form of labor. I will be more intentional about finding ways to compensate students for their time. Previously, I believed that students benefited from telling their stories and that my research would somehow impact the practice of student affairs, thus serving as a benefit to the students. In fact, research can and does have an impact on student affairs work, yet we cannot overstate the significance of research. The reality is that it takes years for research being conducted now to get into the hands of practitioners who will use it. For example, we started this project in 2016, and although we have been presenting on it at student affairs conferences, most of the written articles and books on the research will not be published until 2019. Most of the students whom we interviewed for this study will have moved on from their institutions by the time the written research comes out, so did the research actually benefit them? Did anything actually change in our field as a result of them participating in this study?

Stephen

As a faculty member with tenure, listening to the stories of activists and those they deemed supportive of their activism reminds me of my privilege to use my power and voice to publicly support activists. In Chapter 1, I noted having many dominant identities, which makes it less risky for me to work alongside student activists, as well as to step in to remove the onus from them in improving their campuses.

I am also left reflecting on the low bar activists noted. They often simply wanted administrators to show up—be present and illustrate that they saw activists. This low bar makes me wonder what more can we do. I do not want readers to finish this book thinking that simply showing up is enough. It is the least one can do, but thinking through systemic issues requires more than just showing up. It means, most of all, sharing labor. As a result of hearing from activists and writing this book, I have seen the amount of labor student activists perform. I am committed to taking on more of this onus and laboring more than I currently do to address oppression.

My sense is that students will always engage in activism given the never-ending nature of oppression. My hope, though, is that through reading this book, educators, administrators, and faculty might learn strategies for lessening the need for activists to do all of this work alone, and that readers will see their role in addressing oppression within their own spheres of influence.

I have learned that studying activism gives me a more nuanced understanding of their needs as does sustained conversations with co-authors who push my thinking on this topic. I have learned the importance of spending time with people who are different from me; reading books and articles about Women of Color, transgender people, and people with disabilities, for example, is important, but even more important is developing authentic relationships with people across differences that do not tokenize them or expect them to teach me. This time helps me develop more complex understandings of the world and work alongside people in ways that do not patronize them; apologize and mean it when I mess up; and act differently next time.

Alex

As we mentioned above and throughout the book, context matters. The contexts I inhabited throughout my engagement with this project have informed what I have learned. When I joined the project, I worked as an identity-based professional at Michigan State University. While there, nothing about our data particularly surprised me; this book and the narratives we collected during the project could have just as well come from those activists with whom I worked on a weekly, if not daily, basis. If anything, the activists in the study reminded me of my continued need to show up while balancing my own need for self-care. When I read the narratives of my fellow educators and administrators, I was both empathetic and unsettled. While I understood many of the constraints, the pressure, and the ambiguity the educators and administrators faced, there was a lack of acknowledgement of the power we hold. It deepened my commitment to work with and alongside activists, to use my various forms of power, and to think more creatively and expansively about what support does and should look like in our roles.

I agreed to co-write the book during the second year of my doctoral program. As a full-time graduate student who studies higher education, the transition has been weird, to say the least. By that, I mean I am now a student again, given the opportunity to push back against certain aspects of the institution I could not when I worked full-time in a student affairs unit. Informed by both my professional socialization and academic training, I have a unique lens on how institutions operate and placate. Yet, I have relationships with educators and administrators on my campus that I treasure and value. These entanglements, in some ways, soften me and my efforts. And still, I continue to feel compelled to push back and act up in ways that challenge the institution, its educators, its faculty, and its administrators to be better with and for students. The graduate student activists in the study have given me ideas to think through activism differently as a once-again-student while taking account of the various levels of power that may affect my experience. Through the graduate student narratives, as well as the undergraduate students, I have thought more about how activism may and does look differently at different stages of one's life depending on their position within institutions. In other words, it is not a matter of *if* I participate and engage in activism at my current institution, but rather a question of *when* and *how*.

Meg

Oppression is omnipresent, which means student activism will always be on our campuses. Engaging on this research team reminded me of the power students have to change not only their campuses, but also the country, and they ask for so little in return. Many identity-based student activists are merely looking to create a campus where they feel welcomed and wanted. As agents of the institution, we (myself very much included in each we statement) should be humbled by student activists' efforts that move our campuses forward. Many student activists don't even get to benefit from the fruits of their labor and often suffer consequences, as mentioned throughout this book; yet, they just want us, the educators, to simply show up. We can and should be doing better. We can and should be doing more than showing up.

In Chapter 6, we showed that student activists notice what we are doing. They see the efforts we are making (or not making) to support them, their efforts, and their causes. They know the risks we are (or are not) taking to support them. For a field that hangs it hat on being diverse and inclusive, we are sure leaving a lot up to students. I understand the consequences that many of us, particularly those of us who hold minoritized identities, take when we push back against the white, male, heteronormative, cisnormative status quo our campuses uphold, and I want to challenge this narrative as I think it is a lazy excuse. I have used it. I have avoided having the hard conversations using this excuse. I have also suffered significant consequences of advocacy and student support. I understand both, yet I still call for and challenge educators to take time to assess their praxis honestly.

My son's favorite movie is *Black Panther*. He watches is almost every day, so yes, I know almost every line in the film. At one point, M'Baku challenges the throne and explains why by saying, "We have watched and listened from the mountains . . . We will not have it. I said, WE WILL NOT HAVE IT!" As I conducted some of the educator interviews and later analyzed them, this line kept coming to me. We have sat in these high-up educator, administrator, and faculty positions and looked down on students. We have watched their efforts and often stayed silent. We cannot have that anymore.

Educators who want to see change need to be taking some of the burden away from minoritized student activists to create the change needed on campus. We need to do more than show up. I see this research as a challenge from identity-based student activists to educators. We know the depth of what they could be asking from us, and we can see from this research that they are just wading in the shallow end. We need to be providing them opportunities to ask for support or assistance from us. We need to be strategic and honest with them, but not put even more burden on them by asking them to carry the potential consequences of our fears. I recognize this is much easier said than done, but I have confidence that we can rise to the occasion.

TJ

When I reflect on the themes of this text and participants' stories, I cannot help but think about all the ways our institutions enact violence against members in our community each and every day. The system of dominance that plagues our world does not simply skip over or pass by the institutions of the ivory tower. Somewhere between the civil rights movement and the election of inarguably one of the most unqualified presidents in U.S. history (i.e., Donald Trump), higher education has become legend as a liberal bastion of goodness that isn't like "those" people, places, or institutions. Higher education isn't like "those" fields; we "get it"; we are further along. We get this social justice, equity, and inclusion stuff.

The stories in this book offer nuance to the view that we "get it" and offer us a realistic reflection of ourselves that, in many ways, shows how we not only fail students, but we also fail educators, and consequently, ourselves. We prove time and time again that we are no better. We exist in a white supremacist capitalist patriarchy just like everyone else, one that tries to break the spirit of educators in identity-based centers. We struggle to balance safety for students' well-being with others' rights to hate speech, and we create environments where resilience and grit are not only values, but also required lest new educators not make it past their five-year work anniversary.

As I think about the entire #ActivismOnCampus research effort and the many projects that developed, including this book, what I take away the most is that my gut instincts, my educator knowledge systems, my natural hunches were all correct. The students in this study may as well have been my own. These participants were just like students I have held space with after each campus and national tragedy, or the students I would support during campus demonstrations, and the students over whom I tossed and turned each night trying to figure out how to best support them. I so deeply appreciate the student activists for giving their time and labor to help us better understand their experiences and how we might help them. At the same time, I was a little surprised at just how little they expect of their institutions and the educators who run them, and I am unsatisfied. Educators of every level and designation must make bold choices to support these students. Every day. Every time.

We have a responsibility through our scholarship, research, and practice to ask hard questions and face the ugliest parts in the ugliest corners of this work. It is only then that we will be able to start a shift that brings higher education closer to its original promise of being the great equalizer, as much as our institutions can be. And not because our institutions are needed to be whole or human, but because the humans that we help grow and develop might go out into the world and equalize through equity and justice. Only then, when we create contexts to support power-conscious and ethical graduates of our institutions, might we be able to recognized the light at the end of the tunnel and finally breathe a sigh of relief because it is not a train heading toward us full speed, but an opening to new beginnings, imaginings, and possibilities.

Conclusion

Through the narratives of 17 educators, who were identified by students as supportive of their activism, it is clear that some educators work incredibly hard to find ways to support identity-based student activism. Much like many of our own experiences in identity-based centers, these people navigate the complexity of rules and policies that sometimes bind them in their efforts to support student activists. These educators work hard, daily, to find a path forward to support students in ethical and power-conscious ways. Educators often find themselves pushing back against the fear of real, and sometimes imagined, consequences of supporting students in the way they deserve. Depending on the institutional context, educators might worry that senior leaders will believe that they did not do enough to "manage" students and stop their activism from materializing in the first place. While educators are paid for their labor, in most cases the compensation is not nearly enough for the incredibly difficult work that they perform. Further, some colleagues and superiors often fail to recognize the deeply emotional and stressful nature of the work of educators supporting identity-based student activists, as a result of the connections to social identity, the identities we are unable to take off or leave at the door of our office when we go home.

We understand the complicated crossroads of being hired to do a job and simultaneously being asked/encouraged to do things that are the opposite. And while we understand, we also seek to push people who work in higher education, as we have pushed ourselves. White folks doing queer work; straight, cisgender men in race-based centers; white folks and ciswomen doing women's resource center work—whatever the combination of one's own identities and the role one fill on campus, they have to push. The work of equity and justice does not belong solely to staff in identity-based centers or the people who hold equity, justice, and inclusion roles on campus. The work belongs to everyone from the office of the president and the board to the farthest reaches of each classroom and everywhere between.

References

Beckett, L. (2018, August 12). Charlottesville anniversary: Anger over police failures simmers at protest. *The Guardian*. Retrieved from www.theguardian.com/world/2018/aug/12/charlottesville-anniversary-protest-anger-police-failures-white-supremacists

Bradley, S. M. (2016, February 1). Black activism on campus. *The New York Times*. Retrieved from www.nytimes.com/interactive/2016/02/07/education/edlife/Black-HIstory-Activism-on-Campus-Timeline.html#/#time393_11363

Cho, K. S. (2018). The perception of progress: Conceptualizing institutional response to student protests and activism. *Thought & Action*, *34*(1), 81–95.

Crenshaw, K. (1989). Demarginalizing the intersection of race and sex: A black feminist critique of antidiscrimination doctrine, feminist theory and antiracist politics. *University of Chicago Legal Forum*, *1*, 139–167.

Curtis, M. (2018, June 30). *According to Oprah, all your arguments come down to these 3 questions. Inc.* Retrieved from www.inc.com/melanie-curtin/according-to-oprah-all-your-arguments-come-down-to-these-3-questions.html

Dixson, A. D. (2018). "What's going on?": A critical race theory perspective on black lives matter and activism in education. *Urban Education*, *53*(2), 231–247. doi:10.1177/0042085917747115

Linder, C. (2018). *Sexual violence on campus: Power-conscious approaches to awareness, prevention, and response*. Bingley, UK: Emerald Publishing Limited.

McElderry, J. A., & Hernandez Rivera, S. (2017). "Your agenda item, our experience": Two administrators' insight on campus unrest at Mizzou. *Journal of Negro Education, 86*(3), 318–337.

Okello, K. W., Quaye, S. J., Allen, C. R., Carter, K. D., & Karikari, S. N. (2018, November 15). *"We wear the mask": Racial battle fatigue and the (im)possibilities of healing*. Paper presented at the annual meeting of the Association for the Study of Higher Education, Tampa, FL.

Patton Davis, L. (2015, November 16). Why have the demands of black students changed so little since the 1960s. *The Conversation*. Retrieved from http://theconversation.com/why-have-the-demands-of-black-students-changed-so-little-since-the-1960s-50695

Quaye, S. J., Carter, K. D., Allen, C. R., Karikari, S. N., & Okello, W. K. (2018, November 17). *"Why can't I just chill?": The visceral nature of racial battle fatigue*. Paper presented at the annual meeting of the Association for the Study of Higher Education, Tampa, FL.

Reason, R. D., & Kimball, E. W. (2012). A new theory-to-practice model for student affairs: Integrating scholarship, context, and reflection. *Journal of Student Affairs Research and Practice, 49*(4), 359–376.

Reich, G., & Barth, J. (2010). Educating citizens or defying federal authority? A comparative study of in-state tuition for undocumented students. *Policy Studies Journal, 38*(3), 419–445.

AFTERWORD

In 1999, I started my first undergraduate semester at the University of Texas at Austin. I remember heading to the "liberal dot" of Austin, Texas with high hopes of living my life in a way that I could not before due to clear oppressive messaging from my church, family, and high school peers. The message I received was that being gay was wrong and that I was not Black enough. I was confident that at the UT-Austin campus I would find a community of folks who shared my identities and that there would be space for me to live my full Black, queer life authentically and unapologetically. The first month on campus, my hopes were crushed. My Lebanese roommate consistently expressed her clear discomfort and hostility with my Blackness, often manifested as passive-aggressive notes and escalated to verbal confrontations. My resident assistant, who knew of our conflict, was unresponsive and merely suggested that one of us move out of the room. I cannot speak for my former roommate, but I suspect we were both too stubborn to move out, and neither of us wanted to signal defeat of our "right" to live in the space.

While navigating my roommate conflict, I tried to find community and safety through the multicultural center and a historically Black sorority on campus. After attending a few events, it was immediately clear that my queerness was not be welcomed and I picked up on the message that I would need to choose between my race and sexuality. At the time, I lacked awareness and models of intersectionality, so I made what I thought was my only binary choice and opted to pursue queer authenticity. However, I was met with racial isolation and microaggressions in the few existing queer student organizations. Through persistence, I eventually found community and learned that my experience as a queer Woman of Color was not unique and was, in fact, a product of systematic oppression. This learning was valuable, and by my senior year in college, I found my voice and agency. I facilitated dozens of educational trainings on how to support queer students, and through partnerships with friends in student government we started to advocate to the administration for what eventually became a gender and sexuality center.

Although it took me decades to claim the identity, I was a college student activist and this experience is the central reason I pursued a career as an equity and inclusion scholar-practitioner. I start by sharing my story to indicate my personal positionality with student activism and offer some insight into why the author collective invited me to write this afterword. Upon hearing about this project, I knew I had to read the book immediately upon release. I have had the pleasure and opportunity to partner with the author collective through prior individual projects and just knew this collaboration would yield a powerful and necessary contribution to the field of higher education.

Identity-Based Student Activism: Power and Oppression on College Campuses is a timely book that situates contemporary student activism on college campuses by eloquently describing how a rapidly shifting sociopolitical landscape within the United States, between 2008 to present day, has contributed to multiple and ongoing social organizing efforts within higher education. A critical strength of this book centers on outlining the complex factors that motivates student activists to take social action on campus and how this labor benefits institutions while exploiting student efforts. Too often student activism is minimized by portraying students as being angry or reactive and where their actions are reduced as protests and petitions. Though this is certainly one aspect of student activism, I appreciate reading how contemporary student activism occurs on a spectrum of social action where students work within and outside institutional structures, develop educational content, facilitate dialogues, and provide advocacy development among their peers.

Reading this book, I could not help but feel the exhaustion, frustration, and burden of labor that student activists often navigate in addition to their own personal and academic responsibilities. My journey as a student activist began nearly 20 years ago, and in many ways, my experience reads similar to the student narratives shared so thoughtfully in *Identity-Based Student Activism: Power and Oppression on College Campuses*. Though I had few models of what support looked like, I knew my campus could and should do better. And most importantly, the work to make this shift should not rely on students alone. One key reason I became an equity and inclusion practitioner and now administrator was to improve the conditions for students so they would not have to fight the same battles I faced decades ago. While this book is rich with examples of how the burden of social change labor still relies heavily on student activists, as well as those educators tasked with equity and inclusion work, it also offers a clear critique of how this conscious or unconscious responsibility on these groups sustains systemic exploitation of labor.

Lastly and perhaps the most significant takeaway after reading this book is how it has inspired personal reflection and call to action for educators and administrators. Currently, I serve as an assistant dean of students for diversity and inclusion at a small college in the South. While I have worked as a practitioner within identity-based centers the majority of my career, I am navigating new territory of being "the administration," a shift that suggests I have positional power and institutional influence within the college. As I consider how to respond to a student petition emailed to me while drafting this afterword, I found myself re-reading Chapter 6: "Relationships Between Student Activists and Administrators." The findings of the study encouraged me to take a moment to consider:

- How have I created, sustained, or ignored the oppressive conditions that generated this moment of student activism?
- How has my work around diversity and inclusion aligned or contradicted what students are asking for?
- What implicit biases do I hold around student activism?
- If these conditions are in fact new to my awareness, how am I partnering with students to change these conditions or am I reinforcing exploitation of their labor?

In summary, these are questions that all educators, administrators, and faculty should be grappling with regularly. One cannot claim to care about student success, retention, and well-being without first, reflecting on their own practices and second, showing up and doing better.

I am sincerely grateful to the author collective for inviting to me to write this afterword; this book offers a counternarrative of hope during a sociopolitical climate of fear, anger, and challenge. As a mid-level practitioner who specializes in equity and inclusion, I am often caught in the middle of tensions between student activism and senior administrators. Reading *Identity-Based Student Activism* served as a valuable resource that not only validated the challenges I experience in my role, but most importantly, offered tangible suggestions for action during difficult campus moments. I am so appreciative for how this book has generated deep personal reflection of how educators currently show up for students and generates questions for how we can do better. As educators, we can no longer claim ignorance about oppressive campus conditions nor can we continue to claim that we cannot take action. My deep hope is that *all* staff, faculty, and administrators not only read this book but also answer the call to make our campuses better.

Andrea D. Domingue, Ed.D.
Assistant Dean of Students for Diversity & Inclusion,
Davidson College

INDEX

Note: Page numbers in *italics* indicate figures; page numbers in **bold** indicate tables.